The 13th BANK

The 13th BANK

The Central Bank for Cooperatives

by Homer G. Smith

Published by

Graphic Impressions, Inc./Denver

Design and Composition/Graphic Impressions, Inc.
Editorial Assistance/Elizabeth Scott Anderson

Library of Congress Catalog Number: 76-20876
International Standard Book Number: 0-914628-10-0 (Clothbound)

Printed in the United States of America

Published by Graphic Impressions, Inc./Denver

To all the imaginative, innovative, courageous and capable people who saw the need and whose efforts helped to create and build the farmer owned organizations which comprise the Farm Credit System, this book is respectfully dedicated.

Table of Contents

Tables

Charts

About the Author

Homer G. Smith was president of the Central Bank for Cooperatives from 1956 to 1974. Late in 1954, he had been named Deputy Governor of the Farm Credit Administration and its Director of the Cooperative Bank Service. Prior to that he served in the Production Credit System for nineteen years. He began his Farm Credit career in 1934 as a Federal Land Bank (association) examiner.

Intimately acquainted with the growth of the Central Bank, Smith has written a detailed history of the Central Bank's development from a young organization designed primarily to make larger loans to farmer cooperatives to the participatory position it holds today—that of the thirteenth bank in the Banks for Cooperatives system.

Born in Washington, D.C., Homer Smith now resides in Englewood, Colorado. He is married and the father of four grown children. He retired from the Central Bank in 1974.

Acknowledgments

This work was authorized by the Central Bank's Board of Directors. The bank's excellent records were made available. The bank provided stenographic and typing service, many of the tables, charts and pictures. The bank bore the cost of necessary travel and publishing. A number of the bank's officers and Directors reviewed drafts and made valuable suggestions. No mention is made of individuals to avoid any possible inference of any bank responsibility for the contents. It was clearly understood that this book would be the full responsibility of the author.

Great care was taken to seek accuracy and objectivity. Interviews were arranged with Dr. W. I. Myers,[1] Governor of the Farm Credit Administration, 1933-1938, J. D. Lawrence, a key long-time Farm Credit and Central Bank official, R. C. Mahone, a long-time and high-ranking Farm Credit Administration official, and Bernard H. Viehmann and Dorwin Scott, long-time top Central Bank officers. The contribution of all of these men, particularly regarding the bank's government years, was invaluable.

Over sixty copies of Draft II were distributed in June 1975 in an effort to obtain the views of all those believed to be most knowledgeable. Many helpful suggestions were received. Contributors included John E. Eidam, L. C. Crawford, W. N. Stokes, Jr., Lloyd Ullyott, Gordon Cameron, Harry Chlebowski, Everette Specht, Everett O'Connor, Walter Rubin, M. J. Carter and Dr. Ronald D. Knutson.

Limited circulation was given to Draft IV and in some instances to sections of that work as a further check before completing the final copy.

[1]Now deceased.

The author is most grateful to Oren R. Shelley, J. D. Lawrence, William N. Stokes, Jr. and Sterling Evans for the biographical accounts in Chapter 3 of Francis W. Peck, Samuel D. Sanders, James Earl Wells, Jr., and Joseph Douglas Lawrence, respectively, and to the American Institute of Cooperation, Washington, D. C. for its permission for Oren R. Shelley and J. D. Lawrence to utilize for these biographies their previous writings which appeared in *Great American Cooperators*, by Joseph G. Knapp and Associates, copyrighted in 1967.

The brief biographical sketches of Central Bank Directors in the Appendix was a joint effort utilizing *Who's Who in America*, *Who Was Who*, *Great American Cooperators*, the presidents of the District Banks for Cooperatives, past presidents, Central Bank records, the National Council of Farmer Cooperatives, the National Milk Producers Federation and the American Institute of Cooperation.

Pictures were provided by the Central Bank; J. D. Lawrence, Dorwin Scott, D. M. Hardy, Everette Specht, W. Gifford Hoag; the Federal Land Bank of St. Paul and the Farmers Union Grain Terminal Association, both through arrangements of Oren R. Shelley, and Western Farmers Association through arrangements of A. J. Sanders; Doris Ross, and the Farmer Cooperative Service through Earl Kittredge.

The Farm Credit Administration was most helpful. W. Gifford Hoag provided copies of the annual reports of the Federal Farm Board and arranged for the transmittal of data regarding Federal Farm Board loans. After his retirement he made helpful comments in regard to one of the early drafts. Utilization was made of its booklet, *Banks for Cooperatives, A Quarter Century of Progress*, published in June 1960. The author's appreciation to Earl Kittredge is deep indeed. He was most helpful in providing requested information and in reviewing drafts. His efforts, and no doubt those of his associates, provided a most important check on accuracy and objectivity. However, as is the case with regard to the Central Bank for Cooperatives, there should be no inference of any Farm Credit Administration responsibility for the statements of the author.

Special mention is made of the great help given by Dr. L. L. Boger, who spent two days of the 1975 Christmas holiday reviewing Draft III. His observations were a key to many changes made in Draft IV and in inspiring the effort to go forward with the many details involved in that work.

Preface

The Central Bank for Cooperatives is known as the thirteenth Bank for Cooperatives. Its history is enmeshed closely with the twelve District Banks for Cooperatives, and it must be told in the light of that relationship. The Central Bank has played an important role in the growth and status of many of the large farmer cooperatives of the nation and thus has contributed to the income and well being of American farmers by helping them to compete in a market economy.

This book has been written because the Central Bank is not well understood. The Banks for Cooperatives System, with its Central Bank and its other special characteristics, has no counterpart elsewhere. Although the twelve District Banks differ greatly, comparisons between them are feasible and there is general mutual understanding of their operations. The same is true of the twelve Federal Land Banks and the twelve Federal Intermediate Credit Banks in the Farm Credit System.

The Central Bank, however, is unique. As a "bank of participation" its functions in lending are observed by individual Banks for Cooperatives in their own relations with the Central Bank, but individual banks have no easy way of gaining a composite of the highly varying relations between the Central Bank and the other eleven banks. As a result, the District Banks in general have tended to have limited knowledge about overall Central Bank loan operations, and participation borrowers have seen the Central Bank from different viewpoints. Some were reasonably knowledgeable; others had only the most limited concept of the Central Bank. Some may have had a negative view as a result of their incomplete understanding of some Central Bank positions—a knowledge acquired without an opportunity for full Central Bank explanation.

The Central Bank has only twelve member stockholders. It has an unusual relationship to them and through them to their large borrowers. A borrower properly should look to the District Bank for loan servicing, but the Central Bank as a participant may be carrying most of the loan. It therefore must have a major voice in the credit decisions.

Another special feature of the Central Bank is that it has grown to its status as a major farmer-owned bank with so little need for the active support of the many large farmer cooperatives to which it has contributed so much, except as this support may have been contributed when one of their representatives served on the bank's Board of Directors or helped with respect to farm credit legislation. The bank's capitalization increased through 1974 without special investment on the part of old-time participation borrowers. The cost of borrowing to the cooperatives was interest as adjusted for the value of patronage refunds. This, together with the cost to the borrower of its required capital investments in stock, where applicable, was competitive or usually below market. There was no need for the borrowers to engage in actions other than their investments in stock to build or preserve the bank. There were no means of direct communication with them as a group.

This is not a history of the Banks for Cooperatives System; that would be a much broader undertaking. It is an account of one of the thirteen Banks for Cooperatives and its role in the Banks for Cooperatives System. It is not intended as a popular account but rather as a treatise primarily for internal use to aid in understanding the past and guiding the future. To that end this book includes detailed discussion of some rather technical matters, particularly funding and credit.

Decisions concerning style and material to be included were made in recognition of the availability of a popular history, written in 1960, of the first quarter century of the Banks for Cooperatives System, the likelihood that that history will be updated some time in the future, and the current preparation of a history of the entire Farm Credit System by W. Gifford Hoag, formerly of the Farm Credit Administration. In evaluating material for inclusion, the following questions were asked: Would the information be helpful to new Central Bank board members and staff or others in farm credit? Is the material of historic value? And finally, does it add color?

In this history, emphasis is placed on events as they have occurred and fundamental concepts as they have evolved and as they may have significance in the future, not only for the Banks for Cooperatives System but perhaps in some measure to all of the Farm Credit System. This book deals essentially with issues and moods of the day rather than with personalities.

To enhance the usefulness of this book, the historical chronology is followed by a more detailed discussion of key subjects, basic issues, and developments over the years. Perhaps this format will be helpful both to readers who desire only general knowledge about the bank and to those interested in a more thorough study.

None of the borrowers has been named in its relationship as borrower. A policy of strict confidentiality precludes mention of any borrower without its consent, and this treatise has been prepared generally in terms of the relationship between borrowers and the District Banks for Cooperatives, the owners, and members of the Central Bank.

Many pictures of directors, staff, District Bank representatives and Farm Credit Administration officials have been included to capture in one document as comprehensive a collection as seems feasible at this time.

The book is designed for use first within the Central Bank, and then to an extent in the Banks for Cooperatives and Farm Credit Systems and by system borrowers and friends, insofar as there may be any interest. Hopefully the younger readers and new directors and staff will gain some comprehension of this one segment of their great farm credit heritage. If it serves to help in achieving better understanding or in reaching sound decisions in the future, the effort will be well rewarded. In addition, it is hoped that a copy of this book will be a treasured possession of all those whose efforts brought the dream to fruition.

1

Why the Banks for Cooperatives System and Why the Central Bank?

Even before 1900, a national need for farmers' cooperatives was apparent; farmers required help to establish and maintain markets, reduce their costs and increase their income. However, traditional lending sources generally lacked confidence in cooperatives, and there was no broad reliable source from which to borrow the required capital.

The report of the Country Life Commission, appointed by President Theodore Roosevelt in 1908, followed by years of turmoil and less than successful government efforts to cure the serious problems, led to the establishment of the Federal Land Bank System in 1917, the Federal Intermediate Credit Banks in 1923, the Production Credit Associations, Production Credit Corporations and the thirteen Banks for Cooperatives in 1933.[1]

The Clayton Act of 1914, as it modified the Sherman Anti-Trust Act of 1890, and the Capper-Volstead Act in 1922 reflected the increased concern by the government with the plight of the nation's farmers and the help

[1]Developments which led to the establishment of the Bank for Cooperatives System are related in a booklet entitled "Banks for Cooperatives — A Quarter Century of Progress" (Circular E-47), published by the Farm Credit Administration in June 1960, a booklet on which the author has drawn.

which they could receive from farmer cooperatives. The War Finance Corporation, reactivated in 1921, was given the duty of making loans to agricultural cooperatives, and in 1923 the twelve Federal Intermediate Credit Banks were authorized to make commodity loans to farmers' cooperatives. Farmer cooperatives were given a boost by a report of the Federal Trade Commission in 1928. A Businessmen's Commission on Agriculture, which was formed in 1927 by the National Industrial Conference Board and the U.S. Chamber of Commerce, substantially influenced the passage of the Agricultural Marketing Act of 1929. Farmers' cooperatives are indebted.

THE FEDERAL FARM BOARD DEBACLE

The Federal Farm Board, a body created by the 1929 act, was provided a revolving fund of $500 million to stabilize agriculture and to that end to create and make loans to farmer cooperatives. Late in 1929, the predecessor organization to what is now known as the Farmer Cooperative Service of the U.S. Department of Agriculture was transferred by executive order to the Federal Farm Board and was active in studies of the feasibility of farmer cooperatives. A principal purpose was to encourage the organization of producers into effective associations or corporations under their control for greater unity of effort in marketing.

The Board had a legislative mandate to utilize its $500 million to stabilize farm prices. That, however, proved impossible in a period of declining world prices for staple farm commodities, a time of disaster in American agriculture.

Initial primary emphasis was on the establishment of cooperative national sales agencies—grain, wool, cotton, bean, livestock, pecan, beet, and fruit and vegetable. There followed emphasis on organizing state and regional cooperative associations for a wide variety of farm commodities. Much attention was given to the organization of livestock credit corporations. Ultimately, as the problems of the national grain and cotton sales agencies increased, stabilization corporations were organized to hold inventories with the objective of stabilizing prices.

The Farm Board operation was a financial and political disaster. Although the Board's $500 million revolving fund had to all practical purposes been fully utilized, the fund was considered to have been lost through the Board's operations and grants to the American Red Cross by the Congress of large quantities of the grain and cotton inventories which the Board had financed at a cost of about $200 million. It is reported that the Board became a "whipping boy" for powerful opponents of farmer cooperatives.

Adding to its difficulties was the fact that in organizing farmer cooperatives the Board pursued what is now described as a "top down" approach. Although cooperatives were considered to be farmer organizations, there was in general no appreciable farmer investment. It must be recalled that these were depression years when farmers, in general, had no money, but there were no plans for ultimately building adequate farmer ownership. The farmers who were to benefit were not required to assume appropriate risk, and thus they had no real basis for the right of decision as to policies in their own interests. It is reported that there was a natural strong tendency for the lender, the Federal Farm Board, to make for the cooperatives many major decisions of a type which today would be considered the direct responsibility of farmers or their management. Nevertheless, a number of major cooperatives of today had their genesis or benefited through Federal Farm Board financing.

EVOLUTION OF THE BANKS FOR COOPERATIVES SYSTEM

Notwithstanding the Federal Farm Board's problems and the "black eye" they gave to farmer cooperatives, the Board's experience helped make very clear the profound need of American agriculture for effective farmer cooperatives and thus for credit organizations which would provide financing. As a result, the agricultural and political leaders provided for the establishment (under the Farm Credit Act of 1933) of the long contemplated Banks for Cooperatives System to round out the overall Farm Credit System.

The structure of the new system and many of its policies were designed to avoid a repetition of the serious problems encountered by the Federal Farm Board. Farmer interest and support were essential. This had been shown to be related to a clear economic need for the cooperative coupled with farmer control and appropriate capital investment. Also, it had been demonstrated that a central government office in Washington, far removed from the cooperatives and the farmers they served and under political pressure, could not easily make the necessary, constructive credit decisions relating particularly to local cooperatives.

It was decided that the system would take the form of a Central Bank and twelve District Banks. A District Bank was established in each of the Farm Credit districts under the District Board of Directors, whose members served in the same capacity for the existing district Federal Land Bank and Federal Intermediate Credit Bank and the new Production Credit Corporation. The Central Bank, in contrast, was established as a "government bank."

THE CENTRAL BANK

There was no counterpart for the Central Bank in either the Federal Land Bank or the Federal Intermediate Credit Bank-Production Credit Systems. However, the experience of the Federal Farm Board showed that farmers' cooperatives needed very large loans. The Central Bank was established as the appropriate organization to make them. Also, the Central Bank would help to finance the District Banks for Cooperatives and was the only Bank for Cooperatives given the authority to issue bonds, or debentures. Those responsible for the legislation creating the Central Bank took the position that its heavy responsibilities and its ownership largely by the government as well as its relations with District Banks required that it be operated by a government official, the same officer who was to supervise the District Banks. Over the years, the Central Bank's role changed substantially.

2

Evolution, Development, and Growth in Service 1933-1974

The Central Bank has become a powerful economic tool in the Banks for Cooperatives System. The economic power of the system results from an ability and willingness to make loans under appropriate conditions and in large amounts to aid farmers and ranchers in self-help activities through their cooperatives. The objective is to help farmers build and maintain markets for their products, reduce their costs, and increase their farm income—an objective believed to be in the national interest and to further a competitive economy.

The Central Bank is now owned by the twelve District Banks for Cooperatives.

INCREASE IN LOANS

The Central Bank's loans to cooperatives increased gradually from the bank's organization to 1965, and grew rapidly from 1965 through 1974, as shown by Chart 1.

In terms of loan activity (measured by loan advances to cooperatives) the change was also of major proportions, increasing from $0.2 billion in 1956 to $0.6 billion in 1965 and $4.4 billion in 1974.

Chart 1
Central Bank's Outstanding Loans to Cooperatives
Peak Amounts (Month-end)

1938-1974

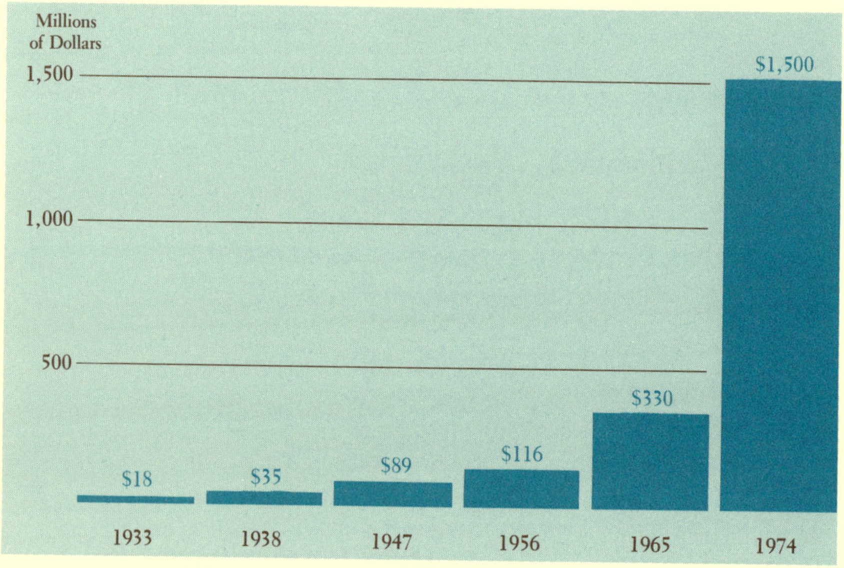

DEVELOPMENTS IN FUNCTION

The Central Bank was established in 1933 to make the larger loans to farmer cooperatives and to serve as a principal financier of the twelve District Banks for Cooperatives. From 1937 to 1963 its role changed on the larger loans to farmer cooperatives to that of a risk-sharing participant with each of the twelve District Banks.

In the late 1950s, the Central Bank ceased to be a principal financier of District Banks, but ultimately the Central Bank's "money desk" operation became a boon to the entire Farm Credit System in money management and the maintenance of liquidity.

The original concept of a Central Bank with large capital structure in the Banks for Cooperatives System was retained. It was deemed impractical for each of the twelve District Banks to maintain a capital structure sufficiently large to handle the larger loans in its district, and the concept of handling the large loans through the participation of District Banks with no need for the Central Bank was abandoned.

Annual meeting of St. Louis Bank for Cooperatives, 1958; W. I. Myers speaking.

W.I. Myers, Governor of the Farm Credit Administration from 1933 to 1938, commented in 1958 that even though the Central Bank was established for the wrong reasons it was very much needed. There seems to be concurrence within the system in this appraisal as to need. Certainly over the years and particularly since January 1973 the Banks for Cooperatives System could not have performed nearly as effectively on behalf of the farmers of the nation through their cooperatives without the Central Bank. Examples include the major assistance given to District Banks and their borrowers in the unprecedented financing by the Banks for Cooperatives System of grain, soybeans and cotton as the Commodity Credit Corporation's operations were reduced, the assistance in the financing of many of the expensive facilities of farmer cooperatives, and the assistance provided in helping work out some very serious problem loans.

CHANGES IN STRUCTURE, OWNERSHIP AND CONTROL

The Central Bank has undergone a series of changes in structure and control unprecedented among the Farm Credit banks. It was established as a "government bank" and operated as such from 1933 through 1955—the "government years." In 1956, its status was completely changed as a result of the Farm Credit Act of 1955, and the period from 1956 through 1974 forms the "years as a Farm Credit bank." However, the Central Bank always has been one of the thirty-seven federally chartered banks organized under various farm credit acts. Thus in that sense it has always been a Farm Credit bank.

Government Years

In 1933, the Central Bank became an integral part of the Farm Credit Administration. Under the Governor, a presidential appointee, all power was vested in the Board Chairman, who also had principal duties as Cooperative Bank Commissioner.[1] The bank's seven-man Board of Directors was advisory but influential. Six members of the initial Board (other than the Chairman) were appointed by the Governor. Thereafter, three of the Directors were appointed by him from the nominees of borrowers.

The Years as a Farm Credit Bank

The Farm Credit Act of 1953 made possible subsequent significant changes. Pursuant to the directive in that act to propose legislation which would further farmer ownership and control of the Farm Credit System, the Federal Farm Credit Board made proposals which ultimately resulted in the Farm Credit Act of 1955. Under that legislation, each of the District Banks for Cooperatives was afforded an opportunity to repay all of the seed capital previously furnished by stock investments of the government as it could be replaced by farmer-owned capital. The Central Bank was given the same opportunity,[2] but it also was reconstituted as a cooperative organization comparable in status to the twelve District Banks for Coopera-

---

[1]From 1953 through 1955 (as a result of reorganization under the act of 1955), the comparable position carried the title of Deputy Governor and Director of the Cooperative Bank Service. However, that official was an appointee of the Governor, who in turn was elected by the Federal Farm Credit Board.

[2]The Central Bank is owned indirectly by farmers through the District Banks.

tives. The Central Bank was no longer to be run by the government, but was instead subject to the supervision of the Farm Credit Administration, an independent agency in the executive branch of the government.

Thus the second major period in the Central Bank's development began January 1, 1956, when it moved toward operation on a cooperative basis under an interim carry-over six-member Board. (The Chairman in 1955, as a government official, could not continue as a Board member.) The new Board had authority to elect a president and other officers and establish policies.

A year later the membership of the Board totalled seven, a majority of whom were appointed by the Governor. The remainder were elected by the borrowers in three area groups of four District Banks each.

On January 1, 1961, pursuant to new legislation, the Central Bank began operations under a thirteen-man board, with seven Directors appointed by the Governor and six elected by individual Banks for Cooperatives—one each. Under a plan of rotation, an elected Director whose term expired was replaced by an appointed Director, and *vice versa*, so that over a period each of the twelve banks had equal representation.

Ownership

Under the Farm Credit Act of 1955, a plan was devised to replace all of the initial government-owned capital stock with capital stock owned by the twelve District Banks for Cooperatives. That replacement, which began in 1956, was completed in 1968, coincident with the attainment of "farmer ownership" by all of the banks and associations in the entire Farm Credit System.

By 1965, however, government-owned capital stock had been reduced to one-third of the total net worth of the bank, and as a result twelve of the Directors were elected by the twelve District Boards (one each) and a Director-at-Large was appointed by the Governor.

Chart 2 shows the ownership of the capital stock of the Central Bank over the years. It demonstrates that there was no plan for farmer ownership until 1956.[3] Then, thirteen years were required to attain that objective through

[3]In the government years cooperatives borrowing directly from the Central Bank were required to own capital stock equal to 5 percent of their loans. However, as loans were repaid the stock was retired. As the transition to operation as a bank of participation progressed, the direct loans were collected.

stock investments by the District Banks for Cooperatives. Chart 2 plots capital stock only, not total net worth. Thus it excludes surplus which totalled $29.7 million in 1955 and $59.2 million in 1974.

Chart 2
Central Bank for Cooperatives
Capital Stock

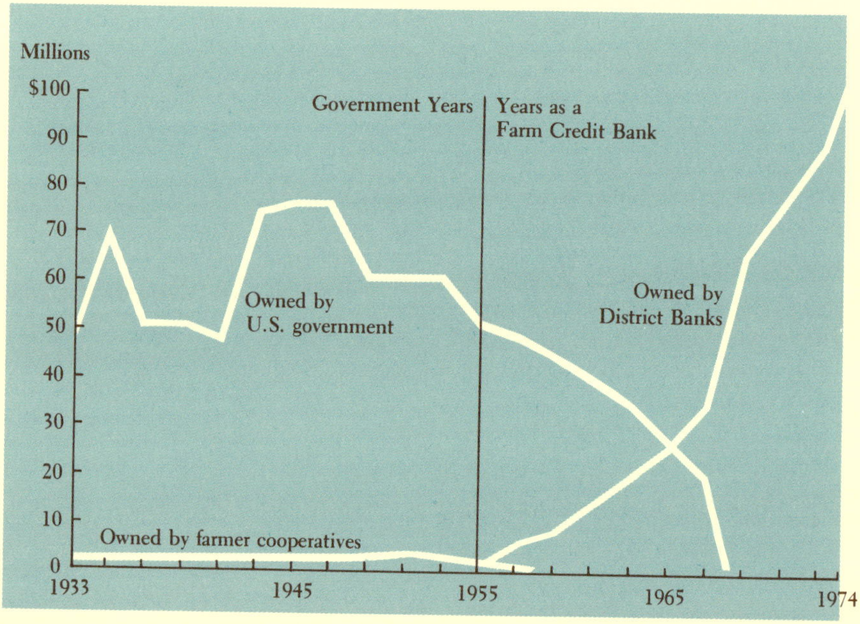

Capital stock owned by the government reached a peak of $76.5 million in 1945. Capital stock owned by cooperatives reached a total of $2.7 million in 1951 and was reduced to $100 thousand by 1957 and to zero by 1967.

OTHER DEVELOPMENTS

A number of other critical turning points occurred in the bank's history. In 1959, the importance of more effective communications with the District Banks became apparent, and a series of major developments, which began in 1968, resulted in the "modern" Central Bank. The following summary shows that the two years of 1973 and 1974 accounted for 33 percent of the total credit extended by the Central Bank and 23.6 percent of the total net savings (or net earnings) over its forty-two year history:

Credit Extended by Central Bank
to Cooperative Associations

Total during 1933-1974:	$23.6 billion
Portion of total extended in 1973-1974:	7.7 billion
Percent of total extended in 1973-1974: 33%	
Peak month-end participation loans outstanding (December 1974):	1.5 billion
Additional undisbursed participation loan commitments (December 1974):	1.6 billion
Total outstanding loans and undisbursed commitments:	3.1 billion
Average participation loans outstanding, calendar year 1974:	1.1 billion

Net savings and net earnings[4]

Total for 42-year period:	$122.7 million
Portion applicable to calendar years 1973 and 1974:	29.0 million
Percent of total applicable to 1973 and 1974: 23.6%	
Patronage refunds, 1956 through 1974:	85.0 million

Other

Total assets as of December 31, 1974:	$1,811 million
Net worth as of December 31, 1974:	156 million

REVIEWING THE BANK'S HISTORY

Basic new policies were adopted in 1968 which greatly changed the Central Bank. The year 1974 may come to be regarded as part of a key period of transition which historians possibly may use as a base in writing the future history of the bank.

[4]The term "net earnings" applies to the period of 1933-1955; the term "net savings" applies to the period as a cooperative, 1956-1974.

First Board of Directors of Central Bank, 1933. Left to right: H. Lane Young, Georgia; Thomas P. Cooper, Kentucky; J. D. Miller, Pennsylvania; Frank Peck, Cooperative Bank Commissioner; Henry Morganthau, Jr., Governor of the Farm Credit Administration and later Secretary of the Treasury; H. E. Babcock, New York; F. M. Hayner, New Mexico; and U. M. Dickey, Washington.

3

The Government Years 1933-1955

The Central Bank was chartered less than three months after the law authorizing it became effective. On the same day, its Board of Directors assembled for the first Board meeting. The Board was a distinguished group, and included the Chairman, who also was the Cooperative Bank Commissioner, a position established by the Farm Credit Act of 1933, and six other recognized agricultural and cooperative leaders appointed by the Governor of the Farm Credit Administration. The Commissioner had high status as a presidential appointee, comparable to that of the Land Bank Commissioner, the Federal Intermediate Credit Commissioner, and the Production Credit Commissioner. Each of the four commissioners headed a Farm Credit Division and reported to the Governor.

FOUR FUNCTIONS COMMINGLED

Under the Cooperative Bank Commissioner, four different groups were commingled: 1) the Cooperative Bank Division, which was involved in the establishment and the supervision of the District Banks for Cooperatives; 2) the Central Bank itself; 3) the group administering the balance of the $500 million revolving fund which had been made available to the Federal Farm Board and was transferred to the Farm Credit Administration; and 4) the staff now known as the Farmer Cooperative Service.[1] The last-named group played a major role in the early years of the Central Bank. It provided an available, fertile pool of knowledge of the economics of farmer cooperatives and was very active in studies and field analyses of cooperative ventures, promotion of cooperatives, credit decisions, and loan servicing.

These four functions ultimately were separated — the revolving fund and the "farmer cooperative service" as indicated in 1937 and the Central Bank in 1956.

CAPITALIZATION OF THE NEW SYSTEM

The authority to establish the Banks for Cooperatives System was reinforced by a plan of orderly liquidation of the loan operations of the revolving fund and the capitalization of the banks from the proceeds.

The Bank for Cooperatives System was given an immediate responsibility of refinancing many of the farmer cooperative associations previously financed by the Federal Farm Board. An objective was to salvage as much of the revolving fund as possible. The salvaged residue (ultimately $186 million) was authorized to be used for investments by the government in capital stock of the thirteen Banks for Cooperatives and thus to provide their seed capital.

At the outset, there was the concept (which has continued) of a large "pool" of capital at the Central Bank. Thus, the initial subscribed capital of the thirteen banks, which totalled $110 million, was divided among the twelve District Banks at $5 million each and the Central Bank at $50 million. Also, federal authorities, in releasing funds from the residue of the revolving fund, were willing to provide one large centralized pool of capital

---

[1]The Farmer Cooperative Service originated in 1914 from recommendations of the Country Life Commission. Later, its responsibilities were clearly defined in an Act of 1926 as a Division of Cooperative Marketing in the Department of Agriculture. Subsequently it was transferred to the Federal Farm Board. In 1933, it became the research, service and education "arm" of the Farm Credit Administration, where in 1937 it was elevated to division status and renamed the Cooperative Research and Service Division. In 1939, it was transferred along with the rest of the Farm Credit Administration to the U.S. Department of Agriculture. In 1953, when the Farm Credit Administration again became an independent agency, the Cooperative Research and Service Division remained with the Department of Agriculture and was elevated to agency status as Farmer Cooperative Service, where it continues to make major contributions to the nation's farmer cooperatives and the Banks for Cooperatives.

of sufficient size to support a lending operation involving large loans, but were unwilling to finance twelve separate centers of very large capitalization.

LOANS TO BE HANDLED BY DISTRICT BANKS

A policy decision was made in September 1933 that all cooperative associations generally serving more than one Farm Credit district or seeking to establish lines of credit in excess of $300,000 be instructed to make applications for loans directly to the Central Bank for Cooperatives. The Chairman, subject to the advice of the Central Bank Directors, was to adopt the practice of referring to the District Banks for Cooperatives such applications for loans in excess of $300,000 as in his judgment might best be handled by the District Banks, provided that no loan in excess of $500,000 be referred to the District Banks. Loans of $300,000 or less generally would be made by a District Bank. The Central Bank, however, was the first of the Banks for Cooperatives to be organized, and at the outset it made a number of relatively small loans. Upon organization, there were many loan applications in hand and the Central Bank made its first loan commitment three days after its establishment.

LOANS MADE BY THE CENTRAL BANK

During this early period, largely the balance of 1933, the Central Bank made some forty-four loan commitments. Of these, seven were for amounts of less than $5,000, three ranged up to $10,000, eleven up to $25,000, an additional eight up to $100,000 and another ten up to $1 million—a total of thirty-nine loans. There were also five commitments in amounts ranging from $2.5 million to $10 million. As the various District Banks were organized, the Central Bank transferred applications from local cooperatives to the District Banks except in instances where there was an immediate need for funds which a District Bank could not meet.

OTHER EARLY PROBLEMS

First, there was the need to develop sound credit policies and employ and build adequate credit expertise. This was a problem for the entire Banks for Cooperatives System since the banks were operating in a major field where inadequate broad experience and widely differing views led to heated personality clashes.

Closely related was the controversial issue of the extent to which "Washington" would delegate authority and responsibility to the District Banks. One area of great controversy was the size of the lending limit on a single credit risk to be granted to District Banks.

Another field for dispute was the degree to which the banks would dictate the details of policies and procedures of the borrowing cooperatives. It is reported that it took forceful high level orders to reduce such actions to those appropriate to a lender's proper position. An additional great need was to find ways by which borrowing cooperatives could build their farmer ownership to an appropriate level.

A GOVERNMENT BANK

It is difficult for those in the system today to visualize the operations of the Central Bank in the early years. It was a government bank with government personnel. A number of major credit decisions were made by the Governor himself. As would naturally be expected, there was participation by high levels of government, including the White House.

It is important to recall that the government was carrying out a sizable direct lending operation. The Farm Credit Administration ran both the Central Bank and the revolving fund, inherited from the Federal Farm Board and with continued limited lending authority.

The Farm Credit Administration, through the Cooperative Bank Commissioner, had tremendous influence on the District Banks, but the Commissioner also had full charge of the Central Bank in his capacity as Chairman of its Board and its chief executive officer. Under him there was a Vice President and General Manager.

The credit staffs of the banks today would find it interesting to sit in on the deliberations which took place as early Central Bank loan decisions were made, often on relatively small loans. Until the District Banks were well established, the Central Bank actively promoted both large and small cooperatives, making economic studies and evaluations of cooperative ventures and also making the loan analysis and credit decisions essentially through a single staff. The bank had a large number of employees relative to later years.

In May 1934, the original Vice President and General Manager of the Central Bank became the Assistant Cooperative Bank Commissioner in charge of the Research Service and Educational Staff (a group now known as the Farmer Cooperative Service). That individual, however, as well as other members of his research and educational staff, continued to be active in loan analysis and credit decisions. Illustrative of this involvement, at a Board meeting in January 1936 some nine of the participants were so-called "Farmer Cooperative Service" men, six of whom reported on the loan categories—cotton, livestock and wool, fruits and vegetables, dairy and poultry, grain, and purchasing.

A BANK OF LIMITED RESOURCES

It is difficult to realize that in its early years the Central Bank was handicapped by a shortage of funds. Its only source of monies at the start was cash which could be withdrawn from the revolving fund. Funds were drawn as fast as possible in anticipation of loans. Until needed for these purposes, they were invested, at least temporarily, in bonds. As a result, both the Central Bank and the District Banks at times gave the appearance of investment trusts. The Central Bank on occasion had two-thirds or more of its assets invested in bonds and one-third or less in loans. Notwithstanding this liquidity, the bank did not have enough funds to meet all loan demands of the system as they arose.

To help District Banks in their cash flow, the Central Bank often bought from them some of their investment bonds or sold to them investment bonds. Starting in October 1935, the Central Bank made loans to District Banks to help finance loans to cooperatives which the District Banks carried.

The Federal Intermediate Credit Banks were a source of funds. Their authority to make commodity loans to farmer cooperatives went back to 1923. They made some such loans. Starting in the mid-thirties, they also discounted, with recourse, commodity loans made by Banks for Cooperatives. Later, a number of sophisticated arrangements were worked out. Several years elapsed before the Banks for Cooperatives were authorized to hold themselves as much as $100,000 of commodity loans and it was some time later before this restriction was removed. In the case of the Central Bank, until 1953 it rediscounted all of its commodity loans with the Federal Intermediate Credit Banks of Baltimore and St. Louis. There was a major question of availability of needed funds to the Banks for Cooperatives. Borrowings from commercial banks starting in 1943 had eased the situation. The issuance of bonds beginning in 1950 provided a long-term solution.

THE REVOLVING FUND

The revolving fund as originally made available to the Federal Farm Board in 1929 was maintained in the U.S. Treasury. Its administration was transferred to the Farm Credit Administration in 1933. There continued restricted authority to make loans to cooperatives from it. Interest and repayments were paid back into it. Investments by the government in capital stock of the Banks for Cooperatives were made from it and, as such stock was retired, payments were made back into the fund. With the objective of salvaging revolving fund monies, often an existing revolving fund loan was subordinated to a Central Bank loan to provide the borrowing cooperative with a substitute for equity capital. In other cases, a new revolving fund loan was subordinated and in at least one instance the Central Bank itself made a loan, a part of which was subordinated. Thus, that borrower was able to obtain necessary commercial bank credit of $125 million, an amount far above the capacity of the system of that day. It is believed that such measures were constructive considering all the circumstances and increased the ultimate recovery of revolving fund monies.[2]

THE FEDERAL FARM BOARD

There was for some years a much stronger touch of the old Farm Board "top down" philosophy than the banks would find appropriate today. It took time for sound credit standards to be determined and implemented. There were heavy pressures for unsound loans and subsidized interest rates. Even when sound business policies were decided upon it was difficult to

[2]Ultimately, the salvage from the $500 million fund was $185.9 million. Retained earnings of $15.9 million were added to the fund. There were reductions of $197.4 million incident to donations to the American Red Cross and $132.6 million as a result of losses. Pursuant to subsequent legislation the fund was reduced by $35.9 million in 1962. It again was reduced by $1.9 million in 1968 as a result of the discount permitted Banks for Cooperatives on the early retirement of the last of their capital stock owned by the government. The balance of the fund at December 31, 1974, held in the Treasury was $148.1 million. The amount of the fund invested in capital stock of the Banks for Cooperatives reached a peak of $178.5 million during the fiscal year ended June 30, 1945.

resist the heavy pressures to make exceptions, and many plausible arguments could be made.

MAJOR CHANGES IN 1937

In 1937 a decision was made to give independent administration to the revolving fund. It was transferred out of jurisdiction of the Cooperative Bank Commissioner and placed under separate management within the Farm Credit Administration. A high level policy board was established to coordinate activities of the revolving fund and the Central Bank. It endeavored to get cooperatives so organized that the loans could be made by the Central Bank. A first order of business was to arrange for the orderly liquidation of a cooperative which was a major Farm Board and Central Bank borrower. That midwestern grain marketing cooperative sold much of its assets to other grain marketing cooperatives and to commercial interests. A few of the cooperatives which were purchasing assets were backed by existing and/or new revolving fund loans. Those loans provided funds on a subordinated basis to serve in lieu of equity capital and permit new loans by the Central Bank for acquisition of facilities and for operation.

Also in 1937 there was a hint of the basic decision which prevailed that the loans to cooperatives ultimately would be made by the District Banks. The Central Bank would participate in the larger loans. Later that year, through the Farm Credit Act of 1937, there was a significant amendment to legislation[3] which permitted District Banks to participate in Central Bank loans and the Central Bank in District Bank loans. It also permitted the Banks for Cooperatives to borrow from commercial banks.

The first agreement to participate in a District Bank loan followed shortly to the extent of $25,000 when the loan reached a level of $525,000 and thereafter in any loans for facilities and operating capital above $775,000, the then lending limit of the Baltimore Bank based on 10 percent of its net worth.

---

[3]The additions are italicized in the following excerpt from Section 35 of the Farm Credit Act of 1937: ". . . the Central Bank is authorized to. . . (c) to buy from, and sell to, any such bank (district bank for cooperatives) or any Federal Intermediate Credit Bank any note, draft, bill of exchange, debenture, or other obligation, *or any interest therein*; and (d) to borrow from and discount or rediscount paper with, any and all such banks *and commercial banks.*"

COMMERCIAL BANK BORROWINGS

The District Banks led in establishing relations with commercial banks and in obtaining lines of credit from them. It was not until 1943 that the Central Bank made its first borrowing from a commercial bank, a $5 million secured loan from a major New York bank at a rate of 65/100 of 1 percent. Later, the Central Bank established its first deposit accounts with commercial banks.[4] Thereafter, it arranged large credit lines with another New York bank and a Chicago bank, the first borrowings being $10 million at 3/4 of 1 percent.

LOW INTEREST RATES

Interest rates were low by today's standards, and today's borrowing cooperatives would be envious of the rates then available. For example, loans essentially of revolving fund monies were made by the Central Bank to District Banks for Cooperatives first at 1/8 of 1 percent and then at the cost of borrowed funds plus 1/8 of 1 percent. Later there were continuing complaints from some associations about the high rates charged borrowers by the Central Bank in relation to those available through commercial banks.

As an extreme example, a major cotton marketing association—later liquidated—had subordinated loans both from the revolving fund and the Central Bank. The association also was supported by revolving fund loans to its member associations, which in turn used such funds for investment in the association. These supported commercial bank commitments of some $125 million. The association had applied to the Central Bank for a loan of $80 million which necessarily was declined; the bank did not have the funds available. The Central Bank later sought some part of the seasonal financing in view of the risk it and the Farm Credit Administration (through the revolving fund) were taking on the subordinated loans; however, the Central Bank's rate was 2 percent, whereas the commercial banks were charging 1 3/8 percent.

In this regard, until the liberalization brought about by the Farm Credit Act of 1955, the rate structure as provided in the Farm Credit Act of 1933 resulted in a rate on operating capital loans of about 1 percent in excess of the Federal Intermediate Credit Bank discount rate, and that on facility

---

[4]In the early years, the Central Bank made its disbursements through the U.S. Treasury.

loans being related to the prevailing rate on mortgage loans made to members of the Federal Land Bank Associations.

In 1948, interest rates charged by the District Banks after substantial increases still were 2 to 3 percent (one bank at 1 3/4 percent on commodity loans). These rates applied to all loans except those to finance physical facilities, which were at 4 percent.

TRANSFER TO THE DEPARTMENT OF AGRICULTURE

In 1939, by Executive Order, the Farm Credit Administration lost its highly valued status as an independent agency in the Executive Branch of the government and was transferred to the U.S. Department of Agriculture. Thus the Central Bank, run by Farm Credit Administration officials, also was taken over by the Department of Agriculture.

As a part of a major government department, the Farm Credit Administration naturally was subject to new influences. There were some forces at least seeking to federalize the whole Farm Credit System. Such developments, and particularly the Government Corporation Control Act, had a profound effect in encouraging a concentrated effort to attain full farmer ownership and greater farmer control of all the banks and associations of the Farm Credit System. They contributed greatly to the grass roots push for the Farm Credit Act of 1953, under which the Farm Credit Administration again became an independent agency.

WORLD WAR II

Cooperatives borrowing from the bank were deeply involved in many activities related to food and fiber and cooperated extensively with defense officials during World War II. Increased borrowed funds were needed for these purposes.

As a war measure, the Central Bank in 1942, along with the Farm Credit Administration, was relocated to Kansas City. At the end of the war, it was moved back to Washington.

THE GOVERNMENT CORPORATION CONTROL ACT OF 1946

This law had only a mild effect on the mixed government and privately owned Banks for Cooperatives. It would not be mentioned now that it no longer applies except that the devastating effect of its budget aspects on the then wholly government-owned Federal Intermediate Credit Banks and Production Credit Corporations contributed to the profound results as mentioned previously.[5]

FUNDS RUN OUT FOR TERM LOANS

By the late 1940s, the Central Bank had established excellent rapport with major commercial banks, and the Central Bank financed its seasonal needs largely through commercial bank borrowings. These borrowings were secured by seasonal loans made by the bank. The commercial banks in general were not willing to accept term loans as security for the seasonal borrowings. The same situation prevailed generally in the District Banks' borrowings. As a result, as loan volume increased, the system began to run out of money for term loans. There were discussions with the District Bank presidents of possible allocations, and the rumor that the system was out of funds for term loans had a serious adverse effect on the reputation of the system as reliable lender.

CENTRAL BANK BONDS (DEBENTURES)

The authorization for the Central Bank to issue bonds had been included in the Farm Credit Act of 1933, and the feasibility of issuing such securities was discussed at meetings of the Board. Finally, in 1950, the first issue of Central Bank bonds (with a three-year maturity) was offered and was favorably received on the market. A new era had arrived for the system, and Table 1 lists the various issues of the Central Bank bonds. The proceeds of some of these issues, as for example the three-year issue of June 1, 1954, were in turn used for term loans from the Central Bank to the various District Banks for Cooperatives.

---

[5]Those organizations were characterized by their very limited annual operating budgets (sometimes less than $100,000), their penchant for efficiency and economy in operation and their push for farmer control through their farmer boards of directors. To treat them as though they were government offices operating on directly appropriated funds—and subject to arbitrary mandatory percentage staff reductions at a time work load was increasing—seemed inconsistent. Such practices, if continued, would have destroyed farmer incentive and feeling of responsibility. Also, the procedures posed a major threat of federal budgetary control of their lending operations which would have destroyed their effectiveness. The lesson should never be forgotten and the Farm Credit System should be sure to so operate that such measures will never again be taken.

Table 1
Issues of Central Bank Bonds

Date of Issue	Rate	Principal	Maturity	Term (or Approximate Term)
2/1/50	1 5/8%	$30,000,000	2/1/53	3 years
10/1/51	2 1/2%	40,000,000	2/1/54	2 years, 4 months
6/2/52	2 1/8%	40,000,000	6/1/53	1 year
2/2/53	2 5/8%	30,000,000	6/1/54	1 year, 4 months
6/1/53	2 3/4%	40,000,000	6/1/54	1 year
2/1/54	2 1/8%	40,000,000	2/1/55	1 year
6/1/54	1 1/2%	40,000,000	6/1/55	1 year
6/1/54	2 %	40,000,000	6/1/57	3 years

LENDING OPERATIONS

The bank, through its direct loans to cooperatives, financed a broad segment of American farmer cooperatives including several of the large national commodity organizations—grain, cotton, wool—as well as operations such as dairy, meat packing, fruits, farm supply, and grain regionals, in addition to the sizable number of small loans made in the first six months. A considerable part of the financing involved the working out of problem loans of the revolving fund. A substantial part of the bank's loans were of a problem nature, and required major servicing. Its scope broadened through participation in District Bank loans to cooperatives, three of which became major problems involving foreclosure or other liquidation processes. Losses were charged off in two instances.

CUSTODIANS AND TRUSTEES

As a basic part of its loan-servicing policies, the Central Bank followed a pattern of wide use of custodians and trustees. Usually, custodians were employees of the bank who worked in the offices (and at the expense) of the cooperatives. Often a custodian had several deputy custodians at different locations of importance to the particular cooperative. Their presence and activity and related agreements between the borrowers and the bank assured the bank of a valid lien on cash, receivables, inventories and the like.

This was of great importance since in a number of the cooperatives financed the threat of bankruptcy was ever-present. Also, a number of loans were collected through liquidation or foreclosure proceedings. These employees kept the bank informed of the borrowers' activities, often on a day-to-day basis, thus greatly facilitating quick loan action when there was a need for funds in the fast-moving activities of the cooperative. On occasion, there were complimentary statements by borrowers about the contribution of custodians or trustees to the affairs of the cooperatives in whose offices they were located.

LENDING LIMITS

Some concept of the size of loans carried by the District Banks and thus the size of loans in which participations were sold to the Central Bank can be gained from Table 2, which reviews the lending limits to a single borrower at June 30, 1947.

Table 2
Lending Limits of District Banks for Cooperatives
June 30, 1947

Bank	Total Net Worth	Limit on Facility Loans (10% of Net Worth)	Limit on Operating Capital Loans (15% of Net Worth)	Limit on Seasonal Commodity Loans (25% of Net Worth)
		millions of dollars		
Springfield	$ 7.6	$ .8	$1.1	$1.9
Baltimore	8.4	.8	1.3	2.1
Columbia	11.8	1.2	1.8	2.9
Louisville	10.6	1.1	1.6	2.7
New Orleans	11.3	1.1	1.7	2.8
St. Louis	10.9	1.1	1.6	2.7
St. Paul	14.7	1.5	2.2	3.7
Omaha	7.4	.7	1.1	1.9
Wichita	13.5	1.4	2.0	3.4
Houston	12.7	1.3	1.9	3.2
Berkeley	13.3	1.3	2.0	3.3
Spokane	11.6	1.2	1.7	2.9

The Central Bank had no established lending limit at that time. Its first lending limit to a single borrower as set in 1952 was 25 percent of its net worth—with no limitation, however, on commodity loans or loans to finance commodities within the limits of government price support programs.

THE CENTRAL BANK AND THE FARM CREDIT ADMINISTRATION COOPERATIVE BANK DIVISION

It is not possible to understand District Bank relationship factors and subsequent developments without knowledge of the degree to which the Central Bank and the Farm Credit Administration's Cooperative Bank Division were one. The ranking officers of the bank also in general were the ranking officers of the Cooperative Bank Division.

As just one example, there were in attendance at the February 1938 Board meeting S.D. Sanders, Board Chairman and Bank Executive Officer, but also Cooperative Bank Commissioner; J.E. Wells, Jr., Bank Vice President and General Manager, but also Deputy Cooperative Bank Commissioner; and J.D. Lawrence, Bank Assistant Vice President and Assistant General Manager, but also Deputy Cooperative Bank Commissioner.

The Commissioner and his deputies had great authority over and influence on the District Banks. These men also ran the Central Bank and used their Central Bank powers as an additional tool to enforce their credit decisions in regard to loans of District Banks in which the Central Bank participated. After taking actions as operating officers on behalf of the Central Bank, they then passed judgments as supervisors on the actions they had just taken.

For many years prior to 1956, credit analysis of District Bank loans in which the Central Bank participated were made in the Cooperative Bank Division. The papers and the Division's recommendations were passed on to the Central Bank staff for review. Finally a message relaying the joint action was sent to the District Bank by the Commissioner or the acting head of the Cooperative Bank Division with a notation, "Central Bank concurs."

NEW THRUST IN 1953

The enactment of the Farm Credit Act of 1953 had a highly significant impact upon the Central Bank. This law transferred the Farm Credit Administration and the Central Bank out of the Department of Agriculture and re-established the Administration as an independent agency under the Federal Farm Credit Board.

Of major early effect was the legislation recommended by the new Federal Board and enacted in 1954, under which the thirteen Banks for Cooperatives could join in issuing consolidated bonds (debentures) which would be joint and several obligations of each of the banks.

Prior to the enactment of this legislation, the Central Bank had financed the system in large measure. With the issuance of consolidated bonds, each of the thirteen banks could finance its own operations. Table 3 lists the consolidated bonds (debentures) issued prior to December 31, 1955 and the Central Bank participation.

In 1954, the first of a series of substantial increases in the lending limits of the District Banks for Cooperatives occurred. In 1955, key legislation in the form of the Farm Credit Act was passed.

Table 3
Consolidated Bonds Issued Prior to December 31, 1955

Date of Issue	Rate	Maturing	Total Principal	Central Bank Participation in the Issue
Feb. 1, 1955	1.90%	Feb. 1, 1956	$40 million	$5 million
June 1, 1955	2.35%	June 1, 1956	$30 million	$9.75 million

RELATIONS OF CENTRAL BANK WITH DISTRICT BANKS

Although the Central Bank's basic role was supportive of the District Banks, there were areas where it was, in effect, competitive with them. The "seed" government capital from the revolving fund was extremely important to all of the banks; the larger the capital, the larger the earnings and the lending limit. In addition, in the very early years before there were commercial bank borrowings, the larger the capital, the more funds there were for making loans to cooperatives. There naturally were running negotiations regarding the distribution of the available revolving fund monies.

The Central Bank was established primarily to handle the large loans, and in the early years, it perhaps was in a position to develop more quickly than the other banks the necessary expertise and personnel resources. However, District Banks developed quite rapidly and they desired very much to handle the large loans themselves.

Starting in 1937, the ultimate pattern began to take hold. The Central Bank would participate in the larger District Bank loans. Arrangements were made for very generous compensation to the District Banks as a means of providing them income to offset their expenses and build net earnings, thus increasing their net worth more rapidly.[6]

In the very early years, the Central Bank actively solicited both large and small loans. Later it was restricted from such solicitation, but until 1953, there was no restriction against large cooperatives arranging to do business directly with the Central Bank.

It is reported that at times the Central Bank appeared to act arbitrarily in its relations with the District Banks, but also that the District Banks may have been overzealous on occasion in seeking benefits at the expense of the Central Bank. Inasmuch as the Central Bank was controlled by the Farm Credit Administration which in turn supervised the District Banks, it was difficult to convince the District Banks that they were always treated equitably. Certainly their lending limits were kept at relatively low levels.

TRENDS IN GROWTH

The financial trends are shown by the comparisons in Table 4 and Table 5. The figures are small compared to those of 1974. However, it should be recalled that loan commitments and activity exceeded outstanding loans and that there were numerous problem credit situations that required intensive servicing effort.

---

[6]Some of the rates of compensation were: 1948-1952, 25% of interest; 1952-1954, various; 1954-1956, 15% of interest. In 1956, compensation was reduced to 1/4 of 1 percent of the principal of the participation and in 1971 was eliminated altogether.

Table 4
Trends in Assets, Liabilities, and Capital
1935-1955

	December 31		
	1935	1945	1955
		millions	
Assets			
Cash and investments in securities	$59.5	$32.7	$36.3
Loans to District Banks for Cooperatives	$–	$10.2	$66.4
Loans to farmer cooperatives [a]	$19.6	$73.5	$76.8
Accrued interest receivable	[b]	0.2	0.5
Total	$19.6	$73.7	$77.3
Less: Reserve for losses	–	0.1	0.8
Net	$19.6	$73.6	$76.5
Other assets	0.4	0.4	2.3
Total assets	$79.5	$116.9	$181.5
Liabilities and capital			
Borrowings			
Federal Intermediate Credit Banks (through various means)	$5.6	$24.9	$–
Commercial banks	–	–	45.0
Bonds (debentures)			
Central Bank obligations			40.0
Participation in consolidated obligations of the 13 Banks for Cooperatives			14.8
Other liabilities	–	0.1	0.8
Total liabilities	$5.6	$25.0	$100.6
Capital accounts			
Capital stock owned by U.S. Government	$70.0	$76.5	$50.5
Capital stock owned by cooperatives	1.0	1.1	0.7
Surplus, reserves, etc.	2.9	14.3	29.7
Total capital accounts	$73.9	$91.9	$80.9
Total liabilities and capital	$79.5	$116.9	$181.5

[a] Represents a combination of loans direct to cooperatives less participations sold to District Banks plus in 1945 and 1955 participations purchased in loans of District Banks. Excludes in 1935 some $2.5 million of loans carried by District Banks on a split financing basis. It was not until 1937 that there was authority to sell participations.

[b] Nominal.

Table 5
Trends in Income, Expense, and Net Earnings
1935-1955

	Fiscal Year Ended June 30		
	1935	1945	1955
		millions	
Income on loans	$ .4	$1.0	$4.5
Income from investments	.9	.6	.4
Total income	$1.3	$1.6	$4.9
Cost of borrowed funds	$–	$ .3	$2.2
Compensation expense payable to District Banks for servicing loans	–	–	.3
Operating expenses	.2	.1	.2
Adjustments to reserve for losses	–	.1	–
Total expenses	$ .2	$ .5	$2.7
Net earnings	$1.1	$1.1	$2.2

EXECUTIVE OFFICERS OF THE BANK

Outstanding individuals have served as executive officers throughout the bank's history.[7]

Francis W. Peck, 1933-1935.

Samuel D. Sanders, 1936-1947.

James Earl Wells, Jr., 1947-1948.

---

[7]The biographies of these leaders in the history of the Central Bank were written by several individuals. That of Mr. Peck was written by Oren R. Shelley, who knew Mr. Peck well. They worked together in the Agricultural Extension Division of the University of Minnesota, which Peck headed. Later they were associated through Mr. Shelley's employment at the St. Paul Bank for Cooperatives. The biography of Samuel Sanders was prepared

Robert L. Farrington, 1949-1953.

Joseph Douglas Lawrence, 1954.

Homer G. Smith, 1954-1955.

---

by Joseph Douglas Lawrence, who was Deputy Commissioner under Sanders in charge of the supervision of the District Banks.

The biography of James Earl Wells, Jr., was prepared by W.R. Stokes, Jr., who served on the legal staff of the Farm Credit Administration and later as an attorney for the Houston Bank for Cooperatives and from 1947 to 1957 as its president. The biographies of Robert L. Farrington and Homer G. Smith were prepared by Homer G. Smith, a long time Farm Credit Administration official who in 1954 became Deputy Governor and Director of the Cooperative Bank Service. He then served as president of the Central Bank for Cooperatives until his retirement in 1974.

The biography of Joseph Douglas Lawrence was written by Sterling Evans, who in 1933 became the first president of the Houston Bank for Cooperatives. He later served for many years as president of the Federal Land Bank of Houston.

Francis W. Peck

Francis W. Peck was recognized early in his career as an outstanding agricultural educator with a dedication and interst in helping improve farm conditions.

He was born in St. Paul, Minnesota, on May 20, 1885, and grew up on a farm. He graduated from the College of Agriculture at the University of Minnesota in 1912 and was appointed assistant professor of farm management. In 1917 he was granted the Master's Degree and was an associate professor from 1918 to 1919. He then went to the U.S. Department of Agriculture where he held the position of farm economist in the Office of Farm Management until 1921, when he was appointed Director of Agricultural Extension of the University of Minnesota. He served in this capacity until 1933, when he was named Cooperative Bank Commissioner in the new Farm Credit Administration.

In this capacity he shared the responsibility for organizing, staffing, and supervising the new Banks for Cooperatives. Peck recruited top men to handle the lending operations and set the tone for extending sound credit to the larger cooperatives operating across district lines.

On many occasions, Frank Peck recalled some of the problems confronting him in getting the kind of personnel needed to head the new Banks for Cooperatives. Many pressures were put on him to select favorite persons of certain groups or individuals, but he stood fast and selected men who he felt had the integrity and professional competence to head the new regional banks.

By 1936, Frank Peck felt that he had accomplished most of the objectives in establishing the Banks for Cooperatives System, and in January 1936 he resumed his position as Director of Agricultural Extension at the University of Minnesota. He had given the needed leadership and left his mark for others to follow to continue building the system. In succeeding years he served the Farm Credit System as president of the Federal Land Bank of St. Paul and as a member of the Federal Farm Credit Board, earning the respect and admiration of all who came to know him. He died on August 18, 1966.

Samuel D. Sanders

Samuel D. Sanders held no college degree other than an honorary doctor's degree from the University of Wisconsin. The award was in recognition of his outstanding contribution to cooperative organization and business methods and to the development of the Banks for Cooperatives.

Mr. Sanders' conventional education ended in the third grade in a little country school in the Ozarks of Arkansas, an educational institution somewhat less advanced than one would expect to find in the large metropolitan communities. Nevertheless, Mr. Sanders came to Washington with a background of experience and a record of success that eminently qualified him for leadership in the development of agricultural cooperatives. At the time he took up his duties as Cooperative Bank Commissioner the cooperative movement was growing rapidly under the stimulus of available capital from the newly organized Banks for Cooperatives System.

It was indeed fortunate that this developing cooperative financing system had the quality of practical leadership that Mr. Sanders provided. The success stories of the Banks for Cooperatives and their patrons might have been greatly different if a lesser man had been Commissioner at that time.

Mr. Sanders learned how cooperatives should be organized and operated the hard way and in the best possible school, namely, the school of how-not-to-starve-to-death. He had been a wheat grower in east Washington state at a time when the small farmers had to cooperate to survive. He organized his neighbors to do necessary things together that none could do alone.

After growing wheat in the area where Mr. Sanders farmed became economically impracticable even with cooperative marketing, he acquired a poultry farm near Puyallup, Washington. He took a short course in poultry and egg production at the University of Washington and began business. He peddled eggs up and down the streets of Puyallup. So did his neighboring egg producers.

It did not take him long to convince his neighbors that competing with each other up and down the streets of Puyallup was not the way to market eggs.

The Washington Cooperative Egg and Poultry Association (now Western Farmers Association) was organized with Mr. Sanders in the forefront. Under his leadership and the dedicated efforts of his able "co-workers," as he called them, this cooperative grew to be one of the largest and most successful in the nation. He was its board chairman, president and general manager. It became one of the most important suppliers of eggs in the eastern markets. Every sound cooperative and business principle was employed in developing this big successful cooperative business institution. Mr. Sanders knew them all. He knew as few other contemporaries knew what it takes to make a cooperative business successful.

As Commissioner, he was the leader in the development of sound constructive lending throughout the cooperative bank system. A sound credit policy at the control center was of great importance at this stage of the formative period of the Banks for Cooperatives.

Credit experience in the regional banks in the beginning was either almost non-existent or inappropriate. The presidents of the banks, who were the chairmen of the loan committees, were mostly educators. There were four Ph.D's among them, several politicians, and others of demonstrated ability. None were bankers. The other two members of the loan committees were the secretary and the treasurer. The secretaries were largely educators, and other men active in the agricultural cooperative field. They were not bankers, either.

In selecting the first treasurers it was deemed wise to select country bankers for these positions to temper the exuberant promotional spirit of the other officers. This philosophy did not work. The experienced bankers could not absorb the shock of extending credit to farmer groups without commercial experience and gilt-edged security. They had no stomach for becoming dedicated development bankers in a new and uncertain field.

Paradoxically, the officers who knew the least about credit extension became the best credit men, with two exceptions where there had been some specialized credit experience. These newcomers into the credit field did not have anything to "unlearn." A whole new field was ahead of them. They were mostly men trained and experienced in searching out facts and developing methods and means. They understood the objective. They knew that it was not smart to lose money by making bad loans. They accepted the truism that an unsound loan is bad for both the borrower and the lender. They also knew that if the money were kept locked in the safe the objective would not be reached. So, under Mr. Sanders' practical leadership they set about in a professional way to develop sound objective lending policies and procedures.

The cooperative banks operate to a large extent in a marginal area. They have had to find substitutes for conventional credit-base components.

Vice Presidents and General Managers.

H. M. Bain, 1933-1934.

James Earl Wells, Jr., 1934-1942.

J. P. Strong, 1942-1946.

B. F. Viehmann, 1946-1955.

Governor Myers, in the course of a briefing lecture, said to the presidents of the banks, "Find ways to make loans, not ways to not make them."

Samuel Sanders created the yardstick which became the core around which the credit guidelines of the cooperative bank system crystalized: (1) economic need; (2) member support; (3) adequate capital; and (4) efficient operations and good management. He was an avid advocate of the retain and revolving method of capitalizing a cooperative, that is, withholding a small fraction of the value of the commodities handled to be used for capital and refunding it progressively in due time as new capital comes in due course.

He would say, "A cent a bushel of wheat won't make or break the farmer but it will make or break his cooperative." What he meant was that the farmers would not miss the cent a bushel but a cent per bushel from many bushels of many farmers would painlessly capitalize a cooperative. At the same time the farmer would be making a good investment in his own cooperative. Under the revolving process the investment would be liquidated in due time.

Mr. Sanders' strong advocacy of this method of capitalization with the results obtained was one of his great contributions to the development and growth of agricultural cooperatives.

Samuel D. Sanders was a developer and an operator. When the development was completed and operations became routine he was like a race horse without a race to run. He became bored under such circumstances and retired in 1947. He died in 1961.

James Earl Wells, Jr.

It was in agriculture—the financing, the marketing, the economics—that James Earl Wells sought and found the bone and flesh and blood of a successful and dedicated life. Here he began as a fresh graduate of the University of Wisconsin in 1917, a county agent of Lyman County, South Dakota. Quickly he recognized that unorganized farmers in his county were without hope save that they would help themselves. From this modest position already he was cajoling, persuading, and encouraging beleaguered farmers: organize, pool your efforts, gather your strengths.

Wells was born on June 20, 1895, and reared in Mitchell, South Dakota. His Lyman County efforts were interrupted by World War I, and briefly thereafter he returned to Mitchell as assistant cashier of a commercial bank. Soon he entered the University of California and received his Master's Degree in economics, finance, and cooperative marketing in 1922. In the ensuing forty-three years Jim Wells carved out a distinguished and rewarding career in these fields — but always with an agricultural, cooperative flavor.

By 1933, after serving with the Federal Reserve Bank of San Francisco, in public accounting, the Division of Cooperative Marketing, and the Federal Farm Board, Wells was a confident, capable and efficient student of farmer cooperatives. He knew their strengths and deficiencies in all areas. The new officials of the Farm Credit Administration swept out much of the Farm Board debris, but they retained Jim Wells. Quickly they recognized his talents and proceeded to adapt them to the new concepts of cooperative banking. He became Deputy Cooperative Bank Commissioner, and soon his principal charge was the Central Bank for Cooperatives–the giant Washington-based bank which was to become the reservoir of credit for the expanding needs of the regional cooperative banks.

It was in these important years that his sound concepts of capital, credit and finance were imbedded firmly in the Central Bank and in the Banks for Cooperatives System. He took for granted that cooperatives receiving credit must be sound in capital, working capital and debt ratios, earnings, and low cost operations. He urged his colleagues in the system to become similarly conscious of these principles. Many did; those who did not found his credit difficult to come by.

It was this devotion to sound credit in financing cooperatives that Wells brought to the regional Banks for Cooperatives when he became Cooperative Bank Commissioner in 1947. He insisted that bank presidents also learn these concepts and abide by them. Under his guidance a new and fresh approach to successful credit extension was achieved.

But credit alone was not a single pursuit; the character and integrity of the banks themselves also were important. One bothersome aspect was the substantial government ownership of stock in the banks — necessary in the beginning, but now becoming a continuing source of criticism from without the system. Wells sought the answers, and soon he trotted out a plan for retirement of government-owned capital from the banks. It was to be a long and drawn out affair, but it would be done. And eventually it was done, the Farm Credit Act of 1955 utilizing many of the concepts in Wells' original plan.

The original presidents of the banks with Commissioner Peck, 1933. Left to right: Hutzel Metzger, St. Paul; J. H. Mason, Omaha; John E. Brown, Louisville; Franklin B. Bomberger, Baltimore; Sterling Evans, Houston; E. A. Stokdyk, Berkeley; Alfred Scarborough, Columbia; F. W. Peck, Cooperative Bank Commissioner; D. M. Hardy, St. Louis; George Lamb, Springfield; James J. Watson, New Orleans; Ralph Snyder, Wichita; John A. Scollard, Spokane.

A caricature which appeared at the departure of Commissioner Peck, 1935.

In 1948 Wells left the Farm Credit System for a new career. He became manager of the Farmers Union Livestock Association, which operated extensively in Minnesota, Iowa, North Dakota, Montana and Illinois. The business was in shambles on his arrival; it was highly efficient and economically strong at his departure in 1957, when he became head of the Department of Credit and Finance in the big Grain Terminal Association. It was from this position that he retired in 1966.

Jim Wells died in 1967. His contribution to the system of Banks for Cooperatives was significant indeed. That to the Central Bank for Cooperatives, which he nurtured, protected, guided and directed, was outstanding.

Robert L. Farrington

Robert L. Farrington, the fourth of the Cooperative Bank Commissioners, had a most interesting and distinguished career as a lawyer, in finance, and as an administrator.

Born in Decatur, Texas, on October 14, 1895, by 1919 he was assistant cashier of the First National Bank of Frederick, Oklahoma. His next position, assumed in 1921, was as vice president and cashier of the First National Bank of Tipton, Oklahoma. By 1924 he was also practicing law in both Frederick and Tipton.

In 1931, Farrington went to Washington, D.C. to serve successively as a loan examiner with the Federal Farm Board, as secretary of the Central Bank for Cooperatives, and in the legal division of the Farm Credit Administration. He returned to Oklahoma in 1936 to resume his law practice.

In 1938, however, he was back in Washington as assistant general counsel of the Farm Credit Administration. There followed an appointment as associate solicitor of the Department of Agriculture, then appointment to the post of Cooperative Bank Commissioner.

When he undertook the duties of that office in 1949, there were disturbed relations between the District Banks and Washington. Farrington's calm, steady and professional approach won him great respect and admiration throughout the system.

Among his notable contributions to the Banks for Cooperatives System was his leadership, working with Governor Duggan, in arranging in 1950 for the issuance of the first Central Bank bonds or debentures.

Over the years Farrington also vigorously pursued his formal education, receiving the LL.B. in 1932 from National University (now a part of George Washington University), a B.S. in 1935 from American University, and an S.J.D. in 1941 from Catholic University of America.

In 1953, at about the time the Farm Credit Administration regained its status as an independent agency, he took a new assignment in the Department of Agriculture as Director of Agricultural Credit Services. In 1954 he was named as solicitor and a director of the Commodity Credit Corporation and in 1956 was appointed as general counsel of the Department.

Farrington was not one to spend a large part of his life in any one post. In 1959 he was called to manage the National Wool Marketing Corporation in Boston, Massachusetts, and in 1960 he returned to Washington to practice law. A few years later he succeeded Joseph Douglas Lawrence as director of the Inter-American Cooperative Bank Development Program, which carried out feasibility studies and helped to develop cooperative banks in Latin America.

Joseph Douglas Lawrence

The Banks for Cooperatives System bears the stamp of many individuals. In a center spot stands Joseph Douglas Lawrence. It was he who was tapped by the first Cooperative Bank Commissioner, Frank Peck, to ride herd on the operations and activities of the newly formed regional banks in 1933 and 1934. He set the pace, laid out the guidelines, and established the basic philosophies.

The choice then was clear: one of two paths must be taken. The first would continue the Federal Farm Board programs under thirteen new faces—a government lending institution. This road already had been trod hard and left in shambles by the experiences of the Farm Board. The program had been comparatively simple: first put up the financing, then organize the farmer cooperative. There was no farmer investment, no membership responsibility—only a heavy inflow of money.

The second road was slower and less spectacular: hold the financing to cooperatives with solid membership, and at least a sufficient amount of member investment. Do this through Banks for Cooperatives manned by experienced, talented and dedicated officials, give them the authority to do the job, and hold them to the responsibility for the tasks done.

It was Doug Lawrence's solid and uncompromising adoption of the second road that set the pattern for the strong, independent, well managed banks we know today.

Born in Roanoke, Virginia, on January 10, 1895, Lawrence became a bookkeeper and assistant cashier of the State Bank of McBee, South Carolina. He served in France during World War I and was awarded the Croix de Guerre.

Upon his return he studied at the University of Virginia, and then, in 1921, he headed west. Jobs being scarce, he worked as a laborer in lead, zinc, and silver mines, as a "mucker," timberman, and loader. After more studies, he was a successful candidate for Certified Public Accountant, and took a job with Ernst and Ernst.

Finally he came to cooperative work as an examiner for the Federal Farm Board. Then came a transfer to the newly organized Farm Credit Administration, and in 1933 Frank Peck grabbed him for the position of Deputy Cooperative Bank Commissioner, where the important formative work with the Banks for Cooperatives was beginning.

After serving as comptroller for a giant cooperative, the Consumers Cooperative Association of Kansas City (now Farmland Industries), Lawrence returned to the Farm Credit Administration and became Director of Finance and Accounts. However, he soon accepted the presidency of the Columbia Bank for Cooperatives, only to take leave to return again to Washington for a short period on call of Governor Arnold, as Deputy Governor and Director of Cooperative Bank Service—which carried with it the position of Chairman of the Board and chief executive officer of the Central Bank for Cooperatives. Here once again change was in the wind; a new cooperative law had to be drafted. At long last provision was to be made for retirement of government capital.

The status of the Central Bank in all these upheavals was of the utmost importance. Some were saying "carve it up." Others cried, "abolish it." A calm, steady and wise head was required, and the system was fortunate to have at its call the good judgment, common sense, and philosophy of Doug Lawrence.

The changes did come. The Farm Credit Act of 1955 was enacted. Eventually the government capital was retired. The management strength of the Banks for Cooperatives, forged in the philosophy of freedom in and responsibility for actions, has brought these banks to the fore as highly successful and valuable factors in the development of American agriculture and agricultural cooperatives.

Conference of presidents and treasurers, Kansas City, about 1943. Seated at table: S. D. Sanders–center, far side of table, finger pointed–Cooperative Bank Commissioner. Going clockwise: Dr. C. W. Warburton, FCA Deputy Governor; Layton Foster, Pres., Columbia; J. I. Sutphen, Treas., Columbia; William J. Harvie, Treas., Baltimore; Hugh Mackey, Pres., Baltimore; John E. Brown, Pres., Louisville; A. L. Stallings, Treas., Louisville; Oscar Pate, Pres., New Orleans; Delbert R. Stump, Treas., New Orleans; D. M. Hardy, Pres., St. Louis; A. J. Kuntz, Treas., St. Louis; Hutzel Metzger, Pres., St. Paul; Lloyd Ullyott, Treas., St. Paul; J. H. Mason, Pres., Omaha; Laverne Smith, Treas., Omaha; Ralph Snyder, Pres., Wichita; Harry Stephens, Treas., Wichita; W. J. McAnelly, Pres., Houston; Hollis Beall, Treas., Houston; E. C. Stokdyk, Pres., Berkeley; Phil Mark, Treas., Berkeley; A. C. Adams, Pres., Spokane; Ira Wight, Treas., Spokane; J. D. Lawrence, Deputy Cooperative Bank Commissioner. Back row, left to right: J. F. Childs, Dorwin Scott, Dale Thompson, Irvin Dyke, S. Y. McConnell, J. P. Strong, J. B. Markey, S. M. Baxter, Martin Fox, three unidentified men, Omar Hermann.

So it was with all tasks well performed that Doug Lawrence retired in 1961 – to a life of further activity. International leaders saw the fruits of his philosophy and action in the Banks for Cooperatives System, and sought his assistance in utilizing the same principles in Thailand and Latin America. Today, after a lifetime of valuable contributions, Doug Lawrence lives on Fripp Island, Frogmore, South Carolina.

Homer G. Smith

The Board's choice for president in 1956 was Homer G. Smith, whose selection was based on his record during his short service as the bank's executive officer and Board chairman in its government years and his work for the Farm Credit Administration in relation to the Farm Credit Act of 1955. His selection in 1954 as Deputy Governor and Director of the Cooperative Bank Service resulted from his record in the Production Credit System, where he had served for nineteen years. There, in a supervisory role, he had been responsible for the broad aspects of operations. He attained a good reputation for his work in developing convenient service at reasonable cost, financial planning, pushing the retirement of capital stock owned by the government, farmer ownership of the Production Credit Associations, decentralization, and the handling of difficult problems under the Government Corporation Control Act and its budgetary aspects as they affected the Production Credit Corporations.

Homer Smith was born in Washington, D.C. and spent his early boyhood in the Panama Canal Zone. He earned a standard certificate from the American Institute of Banking and an accounting degree from Benjamin Franklin University in Washington, D.C. Other schooling included courses at Penn State and the U.S. Department of Agriculture's graduate school. His early business experience included commercial banking and system surveys, installations and sales with the Burroughs Adding Machine Company in Washington, D.C., and three years as a staff accountant with Haskins and Sells in Baltimore. After receiving certification as a Certified Public Accountant, he attained "in-charge" status.

In the fall of 1934, he joined the Farm Credit Administration as a Federal Land Bank (association) examiner. He was assigned to New Mexico in the spring of 1935, at the peak of the dust bowl days. In 1936,

A presidents' group with Governor Arnold, 1953. Seated left to right: D. M. Hardy, St. Louis (the only original president still in office at that time); Governor C. R. Arnold; J. D. Lawrence, Deputy Governor and Director of the Cooperative Bank Service; A. C. Adams, Spokane. Standing: Oscar Pate, New Orleans; B. F. Viehmann, Central Bank; S. M. Thomson, Baltimore; J. Roberts Doe, Springfield; J. Kenneth Ward, Louisville; George E. Prince, Columbia; Fred Merrifield, Wichita; H. M. Knipfel, St. Paul; T. F. Tobin, Omaha; L. A. Crawford, Berkeley; S. Y. McConnell, Cooperative Bank Division; Leonard Wallmark, Vice President, Spokane; Dorwin Scott, Central Bank; W. N. Stokes, Jr., Houston; Forrest Brimacombe, Cooperative Bank Division.

after some duty in Washington, D.C., he transferred to the Production Credit Commissioner's office.

Other Senior Officers–Treasurers

H.N. Weigandt, 1933-1937
C. Milton Clark, 1937-1942
D. Scott, 1943-1955 (also until 1966)

Corporate Secretaries

R.L. Farrington, 1934
J.E. Rolfes, 1935-1953
B.F. Viehmann, 1953-1955 (also until 1965)

SUPERVISION

Each of the six men who headed the Central Bank in its government years reported to the Governor of the Farm Credit Administration.

Henry Morganthau, Jr., the first Governor, was succeeded by W.I. Myers, who was the architect of the Farm Credit Act of 1933 under which the Banks for Cooperatives System was established. He in turn was succeeded by F.F. Hill, during whose administration the transfer to the Department of Agriculture occurred.

During the remaining years the Farm Credit Administration was under the direction of the Department of Agriculture; the Governors were A.G. Black and I.W. Duggan. Governor Duggan played an important part in the first issue of Central Bank bonds in the critical year of 1950. Following the enactment of the Farm Credit Act of 1953 and the re-establishment of the Farm Credit Administration as an independent agency, C.R. "Cap" Arnold and R.B. Tootell served successively as Governor.

A SPECIAL TRIBUTE TO THE OTHER "OLD TIMERS"

Many of the officials of the Farm Credit Administration played very important support roles. Their functions, however, were systemwide, and their contributions would more properly be mentioned in a history of the entire system. This book is merely a history of the Central Bank.

The building of the Banks for Cooperatives System and the Central Bank was to a major degree a cooperative effort. These were not achievements which were "done in Washington;" there were tremendous contributions from the districts. The District Bank presidents and their staffs played a most important role in helping to establish sound credit standards for the system and individual presidents contributed to the development and implementation of new concepts regarding cooperative organization, operation, capitalization and finance.

SUMMARY AND APPRAISAL

The Central Bank's years as a government bank ended December 31, 1955. Clearly, the bank had been effective as an important part of the Banks for Cooperatives System. It had financed or helped to finance most of the nation's large farmer cooperatives, it had in large measure financed the system until consolidated bonds (debentures) were issued under the 1954 authorization, and it had played a major role in the salvage of $186 million from the $500 million revolving fund, a sum which became the seed capital of the system.

Most of the Central Bank's direct loans had been to cooperatives which were thinly capitalized and in serious trouble much of the time, or at least in need of close attention. Much attention was given to effecting changes to develop deep farmer ownership, interest and support and a number of today's top-flight cooperatives are the beneficiaries.

Over a period of years, all of the small loans made in the first six months, as well as some additional small loans made later, were collected, including transfer to District Banks, foreclosure, and liquidation. In its entire history, the Central Bank has sustained no charge-offs whatsoever on the over $2.1 billion of loans it has made directly to farmer cooperatives, and in its government years, it sustained net charge-offs of only $200,000 on its participation loans. The Central Bank has rendered a significant service to American farmers and their cooperatives.

4

Operations as a Farm Credit Bank 1956-1974

THE FARM CREDIT ACT OF 1955

A number of attempts had been made by agricultural and cooperative leaders to obtain legislation which would result in ultimate farmer ownership of the Banks for Cooperatives. During 1954 and 1955, the new Federal Farm Credit Board, pursuant to its legislative mandate, put the finishing touches on the proposed legislation which became the Farm Credit Act of 1955. This legislation would afford an opportunity for the District Banks for Cooperatives to repay in full their government capital as they were able to replace it with farmer-owned capital. The legislation would give the Central Bank the same opportunity, but also would change its status from that of a government bank to that of a Farm Credit bank in the Farm Credit tradition.

Ultimately, this legislation received the essential broad support of farmer cooperatives. However, this did not occur without considerable controversy. The concept of changing the status of the Central Bank to a cooperative organization and the objective of full farmer ownership of all thirteen banks raised serious questions. Were these changes feasible? In fact, were they desirable? Would the cost of borrowing be higher? Would credit service be as good? Would the banks take proper risks? Could the Central Bank survive as a separate entity no longer an integral part of the

Farm Credit Administration? Cooperative leaders successfully resisted, at that time, the transfer of control of the Central Bank to the District Banks, and a number of years elapsed before further legislation in 1960 permitted this.

THE "NEW" CENTRAL BANK IS ORGANIZED

The Central Bank in its new status as a Farm Credit bank was born January 1, 1956. A new interim six-man board took charge and elected as President Homer G. Smith, who at the time was the Farm Credit Administration's Deputy Governor and Director of the Cooperative Bank Service and who also served *ex officio* as Board Chairman and the executive officer of the Central Bank.

The headquarters of the bank remained in Washington, housed with the Farm Credit Administration in the U.S. Department of Agriculture.

Although the acquisition of the new status was an epochal event, there appeared to be very little recognition of its profound significance throughout the Farm Credit System and among farmer cooperatives.

Board of Directors, 1956. Left to right: O. E. Zacharias, Virginia; James H. Dean, Kansas; F. R. Wilcox, California; J. H. Lemmon, South Dakota; Stanley H. Benham, New York; Stephen Pace, Georgia.

DECISIONS AS TO DIRECTION: 1956-1958

Leadership of farmer cooperatives had pushed hard for years to obtain sound legislation, culminating in the enactment of the Farm Credit Act of 1955. In the course of the considerations, the basic question had arisen as to the need for the Central Bank. Although that question had been resolved for a time, it was arising again.

Bank management, unaware of the developing crisis, undertook in good faith aggressive actions to build the Central Bank as a strong Farm Credit bank with innovativeness and forward-looking concepts. One change considered was an immediate relocation to Chicago, the great midwestern money center. However, the Central Bank Board was opposed. However, in 1957 the bank did move from Farm Credit Administration headquarters to its own rented quarters in downtown Washington, D.C., an action of key significance in keeping with the bank's new status as a Farm Credit bank.

Board of Directors, 1957. New Directors: left, Frank D. Stone, Minnesota, elected from area B; second from left, K. N. Probasco, Ohio, elected from area A; third from left, John D. Fehsenfeld, Missouri, appointed by the Governor; sixth from left, Wilmer Smith, appointed. Continuing Directors: F. R. Wilcox, O. E. Zacharias, appointed; and James H. Dean, elected from area C.

In April 1956 the Central Bank issued a newsletter, *The Central Bank News*, of which there were six issues through February 1957. The bank also arranged a stockholders' meeting in Chicago in January 1957, incident to the annual meeting of the National Council of Farmer Cooperatives. Some 246 attended, including directors and managers of farmer cooperatives, officials of the Farm Credit Administration and farm organizations, commercial bankers from across the nation and directors and officers of the Banks for Cooperatives. It was a most prestigious group. Charts presented predicted a doubling of the Central Bank's loan volume in the ensuing ten years.

CENTRAL BANK News

Serving Farmers' Cooperatives Through District Banks

No. 3 Central Bank for Cooperatives, Washington, D. C. July 1956

Debenture Committee Meets To Plan Future Financing

The Debenture Committee of the 13 Banks for Cooperatives met recently in Washington to consider future financing of the banks' lending operations.

The banks have issues of debentures maturing Sept. 4, 1956, and March 1, and June 1, 1957.

The Debenture Committee, established by law, consists of the presidents of all 12 district banks and the Central Bank. Each issue also is subject to the approval of the Governor of the Farm Credit Administration.

The final details for each sale are determined by a subcommittee presently consisting of D. M. Hardy, L. A. Crawford and H. M. Knipfel, presidents of the Banks for Cooperatives of St. Louis, Berkeley and St. Paul, respectively. W. N. Stokes, Jr., Houston Bank for Cooperatives, is an alternate member.

The debentures are chiefly bought by commercial banks, insurance companies, industrial corporations, and trust funds which have need for short-term investments. They also are an attractive investment for any cooperative that has funds that would otherwise be temporarily idle.

Gov. Tootell Receives Degree

Montana State College has honored a native son, R. B. Tootell, Governor of the Farm Credit Administration since 1954, by conferring upon him an honorary degree of Doctor of Laws.

From 1934 to 1943 he served FCA and the Federal Land Bank of Spokane in various capacities. Just prior to assuming his present position as Governor of the Farm Credit Administration he was Director of Extension at Washington State College.

He served Montana State College in many capacities--as instructor of economics, extension land economist, head of the department of agricultural economics, and director of extension.

The "Central Bank News" is published principally for the information of the district banks for cooperatives and their borrowers in whose loans the Central Bank participates.

Dependable Source of Funds Important

One function of the Central Bank is to serve, in a sense, as a reserve bank for the 12 district banks for cooperatives. Thus it is of paramount importance that the Central Bank have a dependable source of lending funds.

The Central Bank, like the district banks, has two principal sources from which it can borrow such funds. It maintains seasonal lines of credit with commercial banks. It also obtains funds through participating with the 12 district banks in the sale of debentures, to the investing public.

The importance of these sources of funds to the Central

Newsletter–Central Bank News.

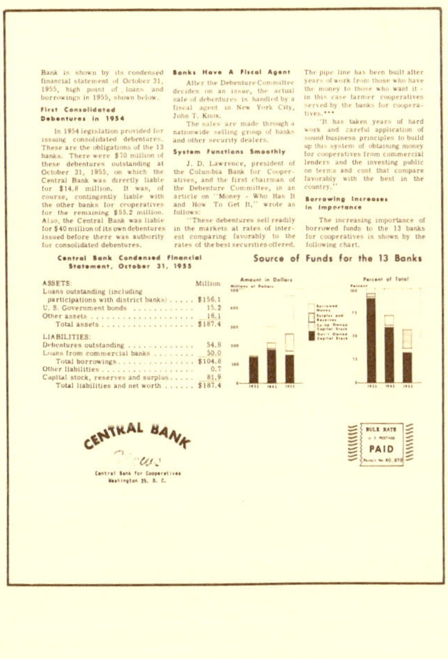

Bank is shown by its condensed financial statement of October 31, 1955, high point of loans and borrowings in 1955, shown below.

First Consolidated Debentures in 1954

In 1954 legislation provided for issuing consolidated debentures. These are the obligations of the 13 banks. There were $70 million of these debentures outstanding at October 31, 1955, on which the Central Bank was directly liable for $14.8 million. It was, of course, contingently liable with the other banks for cooperatives for the remaining $55.2 million. Also, the Central Bank was liable for $40 million of its own debentures issued before there was authority for consolidated debentures.

Banks Have A Fiscal Agent

After the Debenture Committee decides on an issue, the actual sale of debentures is handled by a fiscal agent in New York City, John T. Knox.

The sales are made through a nationwide selling group of banks and other security dealers.

System Functions Smoothly

J. D. Lawrence, president of the Columbia Bank for Cooperatives, and the first chairman of the Debenture Committee, in an article on "Money - Who Has It and How To Get It," wrote as follows:

"These debentures sell readily in the markets at rates of interest comparing favorably to the rates of the best securities offered. The pipe line has been built after years of work from those who have the money to those who want it - in this case farmer cooperatives served by the banks for cooperatives.***

"It has taken years of hard work and careful application of sound business principles to build up this system of obtaining money for cooperatives from commercial lenders and the investing public on terms and cost that compare favorably with the best in the country."

Borrowing Increases in Importance

The increasing importance of borrowed funds to the 13 banks for cooperatives is shown by the following chart.

Central Bank Condensed Financial Statement, October 31, 1955

	Million
ASSETS:	
Loans outstanding (including participations with district banks)	$156.1
U. S. Government bonds	15.2
Other assets	16.1
Total assets	$187.4
LIABILITIES:	
Debentures outstanding	54.8
Loans from commercial banks	50.0
Total borrowings	$104.8
Other liabilities	0.7
Capital stock, reserves and surplus	81.9
Total liabilities and net worth	$187.4

Source of Funds for the 13 Banks

CENTRAL BANK News

Central Bank for Cooperatives
Washington 25, D. C.

BULK RATE
U. S. POSTAGE
PAID

In its early experience as a Farm Credit bank, the Central Bank continued a practice of the previous year and a half of arranging luncheon meetings with officials of the national farm and commodity organizations at times when the District Bank presidents or the members of the Central Bank Board were in Washington.

Stockholders' meeting, Chicago, January 1957. Among those not pictured elsewhere are: partly visible, fifth from left, Marvin J. Briggs, a former Central Bank Director who was representing the Federal Farm Credit Board; behind the speaker, J. Kenneth Stern, then President of the American Institute of Cooperation.

Relationships: Efforts Were Misdirected

It was later learned that all of these types of public relations were highly controversial. The Central Bank was considered by some to be "propagandizing" District Bank borrowers and strengthening its "political base" in the system, and was no doubt thought to be assuming too conspicuous a role in view of the strong system desire to downgrade it from its former key status. Criticism was severe, and a vigorous movement began to build among some of the District Banks encouraging liquidation of the bank and division of its capital among the District Banks. The larger loans then would be handled by participation with the other District Banks. A number of District Banks were outspoken in their support of that approach. However, opinion was divided, and the concept of a Central Bank was supported by other District Banks and a number of influential farmer cooperatives and agricultural leaders.

Disposition of Direct Loans to Cooperatives

At the time of the new thrust in 1953, the Central Bank had some eleven direct loans to cooperatives with commitments totalling about $135 million, plus fourteen so-called "token" loans. These token loans, in amounts of $5,000 to $10,000, had qualified cooperatives to vote in nominating polls for Central Bank Directors in its government years. By December 31, 1955, three of the major cooperative borrowers had transferred their loans to District Banks with Central Bank participation. Two closely related cotton associations had failed to meet bank conditions for further financing and their loans were paid off. This reduced to six the number of borrowers with active direct loans. All desired at the time to maintain their financing with the Central Bank. After extensive negotiations, three of the loans were transferred to District Banks; three cooperatives paid off their loans through other financing. It was not until 1963 that the last of these loans was transferred to a District Bank. There was delay in obtaining repayment of the token loans in only two instances. One was a case where, under an assignment, small repayments were made over a period of years. The other was an instance where the borrower pleaded to be permitted to maintain even that nominal relationship with the Central Bank.

The Bank On Its Own

The elimination of all loans directly to cooperatives placed the Central Bank in the position feared by at least one of its directors in the early years—an isolation from direct contact with influential cooperatives and a diminution of the knowledge of and potential support of the Central Bank. Thus, it placed the Central Bank on its mettle in developing its prestige through effective service to District Banks and through them to their borrowers. More importantly, perhaps, it placed emphasis on a role to execute effectively and diplomatically, in cooperation with District Banks, responsibility in regard to the soundness of the larger loans.

The experiment was a considered combination of decentralization and centralization. Hopefully, it would be in the best interest of the borrowing cooperatives and their farmer-members as well as the Banks for Cooperatives System.

Distribution of Central Bank Savings

In 1956, the District Banks were justifiably concerned as to equitability when it became clear that, for the first six months of the bank's new status, the partronage refund would amount to some 60 percent of interest. The newly enacted law provided that the distribution would be on the basis of interest paid to the Central Bank on loans to cooperatives (direct loans and participations). The total amount of participation loans varied widely among the banks and in total amounted to much less than the Central Bank's capital. Accordingly, the Central Bank earnings on participations clearly would not be distributed fairly among the District Banks. Moreover, a considerable portion would accrue to cooperatives borrowing directly.

As a stop-gap measure, in April 1956 the Central Bank management offered to purchase additional participations from a number of the banks with low participation loans. Some banks responded, and as a result, those banks were not carrying their full lending limit in a number of loans. However, the distribution of earnings at June 30, 1956, attempted to correct the unfairness. Obviously, this did not suffice. The proposal was basically unsound, and it helped to inflame passions. Strong pressure soon developed for the redistribution to the District Banks of at least $23 million of the $50.5 million of capital stock of the Central Bank owned by the government.

Discussions of Function

At the National Conference of Farm Credit Directors in St. Louis in 1956, there was the first of a series of heated discussions as to the need for the Central Bank. A year later, at the National Farm Credit Directors Conference in Omaha, tempers had begun to boil; the strong push for liquidation of the bank had become an emotional issue. Controversy was unavoidable, considering the wide range and the vehemence of the views. However, it proved to be constructive.

Allocated Loans in 1958

A legal opinion had been rendered by the general counsel of the Farm Credit Administration that the government-owned capital stock in the Central Bank could not be transferred by the Governor directly to District Banks. Instead, any reduction must be accomplished by its return to the revolving fund. District Banks would then have to make their case for an increase in their capital.

Thereafter the question of distribution of the Central Bank's savings and the bank's capitalization were resolved for the time by some $24 million of low interest rate loans by the Central Bank to the twelve District Banks. Under a plan developed by the Federal Farm Credit Board and approved by the banks, these loans were made in October 1958 at the discount rate of the Federal Reserve Bank of New York. A year later the loans were renewed for another year at a lower rate, a blended rate representing the cost of all funds to the Central Bank, whether from borrowings or from capital.

In allocating these loans among the District Banks, $12 million was allocated equally ($1 million to each District Bank); the remaining $12 million was allocated annually on the basis of each District Bank's average net loans[1] and related assets. There was an understanding that these loans would continue from year to year except that the District Banks, after retiring their government capital, would be expected to to repay them. They were repaid by 1966.

With these developments, an explosive situation was calmed, and the decision was reached that the Central Bank would not be liquidated. However, criticism continued and the Central Bank was put on its mettle to satisfy its stockholders either by appropriately defending or changing its ways. Many changes were made.

A LANDMARK BOARD MEETING IN 1959

The August 1959 regular quarterly Central Bank Board meeting in Chicago proved significant. The Central Bank staff had carefully prepared a series of many charts showing the financing pattern over a three-year period of each of the District Banks as well as the Central Bank. This

---

[1]Excluding participations sold.

Board Meeting, Chicago, August 1959. Second from right, Julian B. Thayer, Connecticut, New Director since 1957. Seated with Board are: fourth from left, Homer G. Smith, President, and right, B. F. Viehmann, Vice President and Secretary.

enabled the Central Bank staff to discuss the different pattern of each of the twelve banks as well as the Central Bank in terms that Directors with their knowledge of individual District Banks were able to evaluate. At the conclusion of the explanation, a new Director (an influential cooperative leader), who previously had questioned the need for the Central Bank, expressed the view that the bank's problem was one of communications.

Over the ensuing years, special attention was given to communications, focusing this activity primarily on the District Banks for Cooperatives. Communications were difficult because of the bank's unique nature. The scale of its operations and the magnitude of its financial commitments required that it take actions appropriate to maintaining liquidity which were not easily appreciated by either the District Banks or other observers. Communications, however, were two-way, as illustrated by

Feedback by Cartoon.

"Remember 20 years ago when I started buying a little stock in this company every payday?"

"For a cooperative bank, they certainly want their own way."

cartoons which appeared in the bank's records. These messages by cartoon provide an indication of the spirit of good will which generally prevailed and the frequent introduction of a bit of humor to make a point.

The concentrated effort at communications also led to the extended use of booklets jammed with charts and other information. One series which was used extensively at meetings with officers and staff of individual District Banks and with new Central Bank Directors was entitled "Evolution and Development, Objectives, Policies and Operations." This emphasis led an officer to make the comment that the Central Bank was "a bank of notebooks."

THE THIRTEEN-MAN BOARD: 1961

Great dissatisfaction developed in the District Banks with the seven-man Central Bank Board, four members of which were appointed by the Governor and three elected. For election purposes, there were three groupings of Farm Credit Districts with four districts in each. The borrowers of the Banks for Cooperatives in the four districts elected a director for a three-year term. Effective communication between the Central Bank Board and the District Bank Boards was difficult to maintain. It was hard for one man to satisfy all four districts that each was effectively represented. In addition one district may have had a much higher number of votes than others so that in practice it could outvote the other districts. This resulted in part from differing patterns in the districts with respect to loans to local members of regional cooperatives. In some districts the regionals borrowed enough funds from District Banks to finance locals; in others locals borrowed on their own and thus had votes.

The change through legislation in 1960 to a thirteen-man board with one member ultimately (by 1965) elected by each of the District Boards[2] proved to be one of the most significant of all the changes over the years, and resulted in greatly improved communications with the District Banks. It was consistent with the concept of ownership of the Central Bank by the District Banks as attained in 1968.

Board of Directors, 1961. Seated, left to right: Julian B. Thayer, Connecticut; Frank J. Welch, Kentucky, at large; K. N. Probasco, Ohio; F. R. Wilcox, California; Wilmer Smith, Texas; C. R. Sayre, Mississippi; Frank D. Stone, Minnesota. Standing: James H. Dean, Kansas; A. L. Farnum, Missouri; Lorin T. Bice, Florida; William J. Holman, Idaho, Roland N. Benjamin, Pennsylvania; Oscar Heline, Iowa.

---

[2]Until 1971, the election of a director was by the Board of the District Bank for Cooperatives. Under the Farm Credit Act of 1971, however, the election was by the District Farm Credit Board. The two Boards, although having as members the same individuals, differed in function.

Board of Directors, 1962. New Directors: fourth from left, seated, C. Brice Ratchford, Missouri; standing at left, Walter W. Peterson, Nebraska; standing fifth from left, Luther W. Jennejahn, New York.

Horace Smith, Texas, was elected to the Board to represent the Houston District. He died in 1966 before attending his first Board meeting.

Board of Directors, 1966. New Directors: seated at left, Guido Schroeder, Wisconsin; seated at right, John T. Lesley, Florida; standing: at left, M. E. Decherd, Texas; third from left, Howard G. Diesslin, Indiana; fifth from left, Don H. Phipps, Washington; sixth from left, J. Homer Remsberg, Maryland.

GROWTH AND DEVELOPMENT: 1962-1967

The general course of the bank had been determined, and steady growth ensued. A succession of serious problem loans occurred, typical of most of the history of the Central Bank.

As a major objective, communication efforts were continued as the Central Bank strove to keep in touch with and work with the District Bank presidents and staff. Their inputs and counsel were considered invaluable to the Central Bank officers.

The changes since 1955 were reflected in the changing powers of the Central Bank executive officer who was no longer a Farm Credit administrative official. Powers not carried forward to the years as a Farm Credit bank included supervising the District Banks, planning and presiding over conferences of their presidents, exercising a voice in salary levels and in who was designated as an officer, having ready access to district boards in a supervisory role and taking part in National Farm Credit Directors Conferences.

On the other hand, the new status brought the prestige of a Farm Credit bank, ultimately to be farmer-owned, and the strength and facility in grass roots communications possible through the thirteen-man Board representative, from 1965 on, of the District Banks.

Staff Relations with Central Bank Board

The bank staff gave major and continuing attention to relations with the Central Bank Board. Regular Central Bank Board meetings were held on a quarterly basis. Each meeting was treated as an important educational opportunity, and every participation loan was reviewed annually by commodity or type of cooperative. The bank's commodity specialists prepared their reports most carefully and thus gained greatly from the experience. Perhaps one of the major contributions of the bank over the years was that of providing increased scope and depth of knowledge to the cooperative leaders who constituted the bank's Board.

Hosting National Farm Credit Directors' Conference

A significant event in 1966 was the hosting by the Central Bank of the National Farm Credit Directors Conference in Washington, D.C. and Williamsburg, Virginia. A key feature was a cooperative display of posters prepared by nearly all of the participation borrowers and by each of the

Central Bank hosts National Farm Credit Directors Conference, 1966; Governor R. B. Tootell speaking.

District Banks, illustrating the image they desired to project. A ceremony at the conference commemorated the retirement a few months earlier of $3.8 million of capital stock owned by the government.

Central Bank Directors Gain System Recognition

Starting in 1962 Central Bank Directors were accorded the privilege of attending as members the annual National Farm Credit Directors' Conferences.

For a few years previously, they had been invited as guests. This change was a significant development inasmuch as these annual conferences have great importance in the molding of Farm Credit System views and in seeking results desired by the banks and their farmer borrowers.

A NEW POSTURE: 1968

Numerous major changes began to occur in 1968.

The first notable event was a stockholders' conference in Denver, Colorado, in September. This was approached with some trepidation in view of the extremely unfavorable reaction to the "too successful" luncheon meeting in Chicago some twelve years earlier. However, the 1968 meeting was planned to meet the existing situation and particularly the new base capital plan. There were in attendance one or more Directors and the president of each of the District Banks for Cooperatives, members of the Federal Farm Credit Board, the Governor and members of his staff and Directors and staff of the Central Bank. There was a good discussion of the issues of the day. The conference was an overwhelming success and such conferences became annual events.

James H. Dean, Kansas, Chairman.

Don H. Phipps, Washington, Vice Chairman.

Board of Directors, 1968. New Directors: seated at right, Lawrence L. Boger, Michigan; standing at left, Milford M. Beeghly, Iowa; standing third from left, H. Allan Segraves, Arkansas; standing fourth from left, Owen Cooper, Mississippi; standing fifth from left, Chester E. Goodfield, Massachusetts; standing on right, Glen R. Harris, California.

Governor R. B. Tootell of the Farm Credit Administration, fully aware of the problems which had been building over a period of years, counseled the Central Bank Board to take a more aggressive policy role in the affairs of the Central Bank. The Board responded admirably. The stockholders' conference and those which followed provided a springboard for eight significant actions.

Capital Committee

A key initial action was the establishment of a Capital Committee of the Central Bank Board. The point was made that it seemed as if almost everyone in the system was actively concerned with the capital of the Central Bank except the Central Bank Board and that it was time the Board took a more aggressive part. This proved to be a development of tremendous importance.

Greater Latitude in Funding

Coincident with the developing work of the Capital Committee, the Central Bank Board along with the presidents and others in the Banks for Cooperatives System took a major role in promoting new funding options, most of which ultimately became available through the Farm Credit Act of 1971.

Increased Lending Limits

The Board had become deeply concerned with policies of the Farm Credit Administration which were forcing the "proliferation of credit decisions" on large loans by requiring them to be handled by a number of District Banks as well as the Central Bank. A key problem was in the area of lending limits. The District Banks' lending limits had been progressively increased by 1966 to 25 percent of net worth on term and seasonal operating loans and 45 percent on seasonal commodity loans. However, no increase had been made in the Central Bank's limit as first established in 1952.

As a corrective measure, the Central Bank Board in 1968 requested that the bank's basic lending limit be increased from 25 percent to 50 percent of its net worth and that the existing exemption be continued on commodity loans and loans related to price-supported commodities. The Farm Credit Administration granted an increase to 40 percent. The views of the Central Bank Board with regard to the proliferation of credit decisions continued to be aired; this no doubt had an impact on the ultimate decision reached in 1972. On participation loans, the Central Bank's lending limit would be the system lending limit less portions of loans carried by District Banks.

Retirement of Government-Owned Capital Stock

On December 31, 1968, the Central Bank joined with other banks and associations in the Farm Credit System in completing the final retirement of all capital stock owned by the government, including the retirement by the Central Bank of its remaining $14.4 million. The decision required top level discussions throughout the Farm Credit System and particularly at the Central Bank's annual stockholders' conference in September 1968. The U.S. Treasury desired very much that this result be accomplished. In consideration of the full retirement some years in advance of the required time under the formula in the Farm Credit Act of 1955 there was agreement by the government to accept the retirement at a discount of $1.3 million. The accomplishment of this objective required special legislation which was approved in October 1968.

Relief from Prior Approvals on Participation Loans

In January 1969, the Central Bank Board requested the Farm Credit Administration to give the Central Bank relief from the long-standing requirement that all loans in excess of the lending limit of a District Bank—thus, practically all participation loans of the Central Bank—have the Farm Credit Administration's prior approval (the official term was "advice and counsel" or "no objection"). Later in the year, significant relief was granted.

Subsequently, in the 1970s, new but related developments occurred with regard to Farm Credit Administration involvement at the borrower level in credit decisions on serious problem participation loans. Although a cause of great concern to the Central Bank, the issues ultimately were satisfactorily resolved, at least for the time.

Relocation

Discussions as to the desirability of a relocation of the bank from Washington, D.C. had increased. In 1968 the Board requested that authority be granted for relocation, the 1971 Farm Credit Act opened the way and in 1972 the move to Denver was accomplished.

Central Bank as a Full Partner on Participation Loans

As a number of serious credit problems developed, the Central Bank Board became increasingly concerned about the bank's role in credit decisions on participation loans. In 1970, the Board encouraged and concurred in a letter to the president of each of the District Banks indicating that the Central Bank would no longer accept participation unless it was treated as a full partner with the District Bank in the financing.

Permissible Salary Levels

The Board determined in 1972 that the Central Bank would continue to have serious problems in staffing unless it could pay higher salaries than the District Banks for Cooperatives. A 25 percent differential was requested for the President, which would permit higher salaries down the line. A 15 percent differential was authorized. Subsequently, in 1973, in action upon the recommendations of a system salary study arranged by the Farm Credit Administration, the Federal Farm Credit Board granted further leeway through new approved maximum salary ranges. This latitude, together with the relocation to Denver, paved the way for the cure to the serious understaffing which had developed and allowed an increase in staff personnel to meet the needs of the Central Bank. Clearly, the Central Bank was operating in an entirely new atmosphere.

THE FARM CREDIT ACT OF 1971

The Farm Credit Act of 1971 had beneficial effects on the Banks for Cooperatives System, especially in the area of funding. It liberalized the eight to one bond to net worth ratio to a maximum of twenty to one and provided other options both in funding and in the use of surplus funds. It eliminated certain restrictive provisions in regard to distribution of savings, thus making Farm Credit laws more compatible with Internal Revenue laws and, of major significance to the Central Bank, it authorized relocation of the bank. Furthermore, it granted permissive authority for District Banks to reduce the so-called "voting media" eligibility requirement to 80 percent and included other provisions which made it more feasible to finance Rural Electric Association cooperatives.

THE GREAT GROWTH PERIOD: 1973-1974

During 1973 and 1974, a period of great growth occurred in the services provided by farmer cooperatives. Across the nation, fertilizer and petroleum products were in general short supply, and the intensive efforts of cooperatives to meet their members' needs helped greatly in farm production. Surpluses of grain—several years' crops of many farmers—were marketed to meet both domestic and heavy export demands.

Cooperatives grew not only in size and service but in sophistication as well. There was an increased need to help arrange outside financing for cooperatives, whose level of borrowed funds was outgrowing the lending capacity of the system. The banks assumed the role of lenders in leverage lease financing. Additional rural electric cooperatives became borrowers with Central Bank participation in one instance.

The Central Bank was also successful in adding some key officers to its staff and in stepping up its programs of staff development. Major progress was made in the solution of serious problem loan situations. Obtaining higher prices for fertilizer was instrumental in two instances. It also is clear, however, that the years of patient yet aggressive and at times courageous loan servicing in cooperation with District Banks had paid big dividends. The bank's credit posture was good. Its overall record after some forty-two years of operation, both in credit service and in nominal loan charge-offs, was regarded as enviable by a number of leaders in the nation's financial community.

TRENDS IN GROWTH

Trends in assets, liabilities and capital as well as income, expenses and net savings are shown in Tables 6, 7, and 8.

Table 6
Trends in Income, Expenses and Net Savings
1957-1974

	Fiscal Year Ended June 30		
	1957[a]	1965	1974
		millions	
Income on participations and loans	$4.9	$12.2	$ 97.4
Income from investments	.4	0.5	16.4
Total income	$5.3	$12.7	$113.8
Cost of borrowed funds	$3.0	$ 7.9	$ 93.8
Compensation expenses payable to District Banks for servicing loans	.2	0.6	
Operating expenses	.2	0.4	1.3
Adjustment of reserve for losses	.1	0.4	2.9
Total expenses	$3.5	$ 9.3	$ 98.0
Net savings[b]	$1.8	$ 3.4	$ 15.8
Patronage refunds			
Total net savings of Central Bank during the 19 years as a Farm Credit Bank (1956-74)			$ 93.1
Less: Franchise tax to the U.S. Government, 1956-68[c]			7.3
Net			$ 85.8
Dividends paid on Class B "Investment stock"[d] (largely to District Banks)			$ 0.8
Patronage refunds including allocations of surplus:			
Portion constituting income to District Banks for Cooperatives		$84.3	
Portion representing patronage on direct loans to cooperatives (in early years)		0.7	$85.0
			$85.8
Patronage as a per cent of interest received on loans to cooperatives (primarily participation loans)			17%

[a] The first twelve-month fiscal year as a Farm Credit bank.

[b] The "net savings" in large part were owned by the District Banks based on interest paid to the Central Bank on participation loans. They result in a reduction of interest.

[c] The franchise tax by law was in lieu of dividends on the investment of the government in capital stock. Additional franchise tax of $907,000 was paid applicable to the years as a government bank (July 1, 1954 through December 31, 1955) pursuant to the Farm Credit Act of 1953.

[d] This was the only class of stock paying dividends which the Central Bank had ever issued.

Table 7
Trends in Assets, Liabilities and Capital
1955-1974

	December 31		
	1955	1965	1974
		millions	
Assets			
Cash, interest bearing amounts due from commercial banks and investments	$ 36.3	$ 25.4	$ 171.1
Loans to other Farm Credit banks[a]	$ 66.4	$ 29.8	$ 115.0
Loans to farmer cooperatives and accrued interest receivable[b]	$ 77.3	$316.8	$1,533.4
Less: Reserve for losses	.8	2.8	13.8
Net	$ 76.5	$314.0	$1,519.6
Other assets	$ 2.3	$ .9	$ 5.6
Total Assets	$181.5	$370.1	$1,811.3
Liabilities and Capital			
Borrowings:			
Other Farm Credit banks	$ —	$ 8.0	$ 57.8
Commercial banks	45.0	3.0	—
Bonds	54.8	265.0	1,560.0
Total	$ 99.8	$276.0	$1,617.8
Other liabilities	0.8	2.7	37.2
Total liabilities	$100.6	$278.7	$1,655.0
Capital accounts			
Capital stock owned by:			
U.S. Government	$ 50.5	$ 27.4	$ —
Cooperatives	$ 0.7	—	—
District Banks for Cooperatives	—	26.0	97.1
Total	$ 51.2	$ 53.4	$ 97.1
Surplus, reserved	29.7	29.7	29.7
Surplus, allocated	—	6.6	13.5
Surplus, other	—	—	6.6
Undistributed savings	—	1.7	9.4
Total capital accounts	$ 80.9	$ 91.4	$ 156.3
Total liabilities and capital	$181.5	$370.1	$1,811.3

[a] Represented in 1955 loans to help finance District Banks for Cooperatives and in 1974 "money desk" loans to Farm Credit banks.

[b] In 1965 and 1974 represented participation in District Bank loans. In 1955 included some loans direct to cooperatives.

Table 8
Growth of the Central Bank Compared with
the Entire Banks for Cooperatives System
1956-1974

Years Ended June 30	1956	1962	1968	1974	Six Month Period Ended Dec. 31, 1974[a]
			millions		
Loans made to farmer cooperatives preceding 12 months					
Central Bank	$206	$295	$ 812	$3,556	$2,436
Cooperative Bank System in total	$567	$860	$1,791	$6,759	$4,508
Peak month-end loans outstanding to cooperatives during year					
Central Bank	$ 92	$165	$ 536	$1,180	$1,500
Cooperative Bank System in total	$389	$730	$1,597	$3,211	$3,598
Loans outstanding to farmer cooperatives at end of year					
Central Bank	$ 71	$143	$ 405	$ 920	$1,500
Cooperative Bank System in total	$349	$692	$1,454	$2,733	$3,575
Total net worth[b]					
Central Bank	$ 83	$ 86	$ 91	$ 150	$ 156
Cooperative Bank System in total	$257	$267	$ 275	$ 392	$ 416

[a] Not comparable with annual figures since loans made are for only six months; outstanding loans are at time of approaching seasonal peak whereas June figures are at a seasonal low period.

[b] From December 31, 1955 until December 31, 1968, most capital funds generated were utilized to repay capital stock owned by the U.S. Government; thus growth in net worth was slow.

A PRODUCT OF TEAMWORK

Many major differences in point of view occurred over the years, and the results attained by the Central Bank were possible only because of the spirit of teamwork among the thirteen banks under the supervision of the Farm Credit Administration.

A vital forum for exchange of views was provided by periodic conferences arranged and largely conducted by the Farm Credit Administration and called "Presidents Conferences." Over the years, many committees of presidents helped to develop insights and solve problems. Examples of contributions include the now quite universal "variable interest rate" and the most constructive pattern of six-month bonds (debentures) as a basic financing medium.

THE STAFF WHICH OPERATED THE BANK

During the years as a Farm Credit bank the function of operating the bank was carried out by a very few individuals under the President, who was the chief executive officer. During much of this time the bank was seriously understaffed, and especially heavy loads were carried by a few individuals.

THE BANKS' SALARIED OFFICERS AND CERTAIN KEY EMPLOYEES

Bernard F. Viehmann

Mr. Viehmann was the clear choice of the Central Bank Board for the office of vice president and secretary. He served effectively as the second officer of the bank from January 1, 1956 until his retirement in 1965.

He had a law degree and was a member of the District of Columbia bar. After considerable business experience he was employed in 1931 with the Emergency Crop Loan Office of the U.S. Department of Agriculture. That office was transferred to the Farm Credit Administration, and in time "Barney" was in charge of the revolving fund. In 1946 he became vice president and general manager of the Central Bank.

Dorwin Scott

Mr. Scott was another clear choice of the Board in 1956 for the office of vice president and treasurer, the third ranking of the bank's officers. He

Caricature prepared in 1961 on the retirement of J. D. Lawrence. This indicates the high respect in which he was held and the spirit of camaraderie among the thirteen presidents. From top to bottom: J. D. Lawrence, D. M. Hardy, St. Louis, on left; A. C. Adams, Spokane, on right; L. A. Crawford, Berkeley; Homer G. Smith, Central Bank; W. J. McAnelly, Houston; Edward F. Chavanne, New Orleans; R. B. Jones, Baltimore, on left; J. Roberts Doe, Springfield, on right; J. Kenneth Ward, Louisville; Lloyd Ullyott, St. Paul; John E. Eidam, Omaha; and J. R. Williams, Wichita.

Group at retirement party for J. D. Lawrence, 1961. Speaking: R. L. Farrington. In the group were close friends of the Central Bank, including, in the distant row, left to right: H. T. Mason, Deputy Governor; J. Mahlon Selby, Assistant to the Governor; Lyman S. Hulbert, formerly Farm Credit Administration legal counsel who had served for years, in effect, as the general counsel of the Central Bank; in the near row, second from left, John Bagwell, General Counsel, Farm Credit Administration; Robert Hope, Counsel, Columbia Bank for Cooperatives; John E. Eidam, Omaha; R. C. Ferguson, a top Farm Credit Administration finance officer; and to the left of Mr. Farrington, J. B. Jones, Secretary of the Baltimore Bank for Cooperatives.

Group at Presidents' Conference, New York City, 1965. Seated, left to right: R. H. McDougall, Columbia; Neal F. Pendleton, New Orleans; Russell Boniface, St. Louis; Lloyd Ullyott, St. Paul; John E. Eidam, Omaha; J. R. Williams, Wichita. Standing: R. B. Jones, Baltimore; John Rhein, Houston; Gordon Cameron, Springfield; J. Kenneth Ward, Louisville; M. J. Carter, Spokane; L. A. Crawford, Berkeley; Homer G. Smith, Central Bank.

had attended the U.S. Naval Academy and had an outstanding background in the Banks for Cooperatives System, going back to the organization days. He was one of the coordinators from the Commissioner's office who worked with District Banks in developing and helping them adopt sound credit policies. In time he attained a reputation as one of the very capable credit officers in the system. "Scottie" became treasurer of the Central Bank in 1943. In the tradition of the day, in addition to the financial responsibilities, that was the credit office of the bank. As the magnitude of the bank's financial operations increased he was at times referred to as "Chief Wampum." Bad health caught up with him and he retired in 1966.

S. P. Hopkins

Phil, as he is called, was one of the stalwarts on the bank's staff in 1956. He was born and raised in central Mississippi in an agricultural community. He grew cotton for several years and was a member of the Future Farmers of America and 4-H. He earned a bachelor's degree in accounting and commercial law from Benjamin Franklin University in Washington, D.C. He attended Mississippi State University for two and one-half years and took courses from LaSalle Extension University and numerous management courses and seminars. He was employed in the Farm Credit System in 1941 and joined the staff of the Central Bank in 1948, where he gained experience in all phases of the bank's work. He was an assistant vice president, treasurer, and since 1971 has been corporate secretary. He served for four years in the U.S. Army in World War II and for twenty-three years as an active duty reservist, retiring with the rank of lieutenant colonel.

Robert W. Finn

Bob, as he is called, was another of the promising young men on the bank's staff in 1956, having first come to the bank in 1951. He is a native of Boston. After serving in the South Pacific during World War II, he completed his formal education at George Washington University and Southeastern University, where he received a degree in accounting. He came up through the ranks to be named treasurer in 1971. He had a key role in developing the bank's capability in finance which served it so well, particularly in 1973, and its smooth financing over many years.

A. N. Morrison

"Andy," Farm Credit Administration employee from 1939, transferred from Federal Land Bank work to the Central Bank in 1951. He had an accounting degree from Benjamin Franklin University. He was one of the bank's dedicated and industrious officers. Over a twenty-one year period he served in all three of the bank's major functions and completed his duty as assistant treasurer and assistant secretary. He served in the U.S. Navy in World War II. He elected not to move to Denver and retired in 1972.

Lee McDonald

Lee, a Penn State graduate, joined the bank about 1950. His background included work in grain inspection in the Midwest. He served as assistant secretary. In the late 1950s he transferred to the Farm Credit Administration's Examination Division.

Fletcher B. Mills

In 1956 the bank clearly needed a top "trouble shooter." Fletcher Mills was the man. He possessed a solid background as a public accountant, having worked for years for farmers' cooperatives in the Midwest. He worked successively as comptroller for Wisconsin Farmco (later absorbed by FS Services, Bloomington, Ill.), as comptroller of the cooperative now known as Farmland Industries, Kansas City, and as the financial officer for Coble Dairies, Lexington, N.C. Upon joining the staff of the bank, "Fletch" soon found two problems—one a direct Central Bank loan, one a participation loan—where his outstanding talents served the banks and the borrowers well indeed. In 1963 he became a vice president. He retired in 1966 and moved to Florida.

Thomas E. Hall

In 1962 loan volume was beginning to grow more rapidly and there were reasons to believe that this would accelerate. Participation loans to grain cooperatives were a most important segment of the bank's business. Tom Hall was employed as a member of the staff, and in 1965 he was promoted to the office of secretary. In 1967 he became a vice president as well.

Group at Presidents' Conference, New Orleans, 1967. Standing, left to right: John E. Eidam, Omaha; J. R. Williams, Wichita; Lloyd Ullyott, St. Paul; Walter Verlander, New Orleans; Noel Stocker, Farm Credit Administration. Seated: John Rhein, Houston; Walter Rubin, Berkeley; M. J. Carter, Spokane; Homer G. Smith, Central Bank; Governor R. B. Tootell; Deputy Director R. C. Mahone, Farm Credit Administration; Glenn E. Heitz, Deputy Governor and Director of the Cooperative Bank Service; Russell Boniface, St. Louis; Sam Davis, Farm Credit Administration; Howell Hughes, Springfield; R. B. Jones, Baltimore; Robert H. McDougall, Columbia; Wilson Orr, Louisville.

Group at Presidents' Conference, Spokane, 1971. Seated, left to right: Jack R. Cobb, Baltimore, Richard Bonney, Columbia; Donald E. Roark, Deputy Governor and Director of the Cooperative Bank Service; Thomas E. Farr, Louisville; Walter Verlander, New Orleans; Harry Chlebowski, St. Louis. Standing: J. R. Williams, Wichita; Homer G. Smith, Central Bank; M. J. Carter, Spokane; Howell Hughes, Springfield; Hugh Cox, Omaha; Murrell Rogers, Houston; B. H. Schulte, Berkeley; Oren Shelley, St. Paul. Presidents who subsequently have taken office and are included in other pictures: John Harling, Omaha; William C. Pendered, Berkeley; and Jack Hughes, Houston; and Burgee Amdahl, St. Paul.

Tom earned a master's degree in agricultural economics from Kansas State University, and subsequently gained experience as an extension specialist in marketing and as a county agent at Liberal, Kansas. He had served as an assistant manager of a local grain cooperative under James H. Dean and had been employed in a regional grain cooperative as manager of the Service and Information Department. In 1949 he became chief of the Grain Branch of the Farmer Cooperative Service in the U.S. Department of Agriculture and in 1956 chief of the Crops Marketing and Utilization Branch of the Federal Extension Service. He then became an officer of the Central Bank. He retired in 1972, and died in 1976.

Robert P. Simpson

In 1965, as Dorwin Scott's health was failing, a very capable credit officer with solid District Bank experience was urgently needed. After a thorough canvas, "Bob" was employed as a vice president. He had been educated at Lockyears Business College in Evansville, Illinois and earned a bachelor's degree in agricultural economics from the University of

There was fun along the way: presidents and wives at Presidents' Conference, Wisconsin, 1969.

California. He served nearly four years in the U.S. Army in World War II and retired from the reserve as a lieutenant colonel. After varied business experience he worked for fifteen years at the Berkeley Bank for Cooperatives, becoming its treasurer. In 1966 he decided to resign and return to California.

Mrs. Frances L. Fair

Mrs. Fair who was from Freeport, Pennsylvania, had varied experience including work with two public accounting firms and as a bookkeeper. She joined the staff of the Central Bank in 1965 and became its accountant late in 1974.

Hartwell A. Gilliard

The bank had taken the view that its credit staff should be recruited largely from the District Banks. There was good evidence that it was easier for a young man to gain quickly a breadth of credit experience by initial exposure there. But "Andy" had an excellent educational background and was available. For perhaps the very first time, the bank hired a trainee in 1966 for a position as officer—Andy Gilliard from Lamont, Florida. He was educated in both the School of Business and the College of Agriculture at the University of Florida, and had earned a master's degree in agricultural economics. He served with the U.S. Army in security assignments from 1956 to 1960. After broad experience in the various departments of the bank he was promoted to the position of assistant vice president in the Credit Department in 1972. The "trainee program" had been a resounding success. Mr. Gilliard was one of the "gallant four" that manned the Credit Department in 1972. He played a key role in the extensive sugar financing that year.

Robert L. Metzger

In 1966, there was no question whatsoever as to the need to further strengthen the credit staff. Mr. Metzger (son of the late Hutzel Metzger, the first president of the St. Paul Bank for Cooperatives) was selected as a vice president. Before Mr. Metzger really settled down to his new duties, Mr. Simpson resigned.

Mr. Metzger was born in Washington, D.C. and raised in Minnesota. Following two years of U.S. Navy service he graduated from the University of Minnesota in 1949 with bachelor's degrees in business administration and electrical engineering. Subsequent to graduation, he served with a large corporate public utility in Michigan in engineering and administrative positions before joining the staff of the St. Paul Bank for Cooperatives in 1952 as a business analyst. Except for a short period of graduate work at the University of Texas, he was employed by the St. Paul bank for fourteen years in various capacities. He became treasurer in 1959 and had overall responsibility for the Credit and Fiscal Departments in that post when he joined the Central Bank. He headed the Central Bank Credit Department as vice president, subsequently as senior vice president and

Group conference of secretaries of District Banks, 1960. Seated, left to right: Daniel S. Weybright, Jr., Baltimore; Russell Boniface, St. Louis; J. B. Jones, Baltimore; Kaare Rosenberg, St. Paul; Henry Guthrie, Houston; Earnest B. Schulz, Spokane; Gilbert Terpening, Wichita. Standing: Glenn E. Heitz, Deputy Governor and Director of the Cooperative Bank Service; William Pettit, Columbia; Maxey Love, Columbia; Chuck Bowman, Springfield; Walter Verlander, New Orleans; Ferd C. Steuve, Louisville; Lloyd E. Sherman, Omaha; Stanley Dreyer, St. Paul; Fred Ringham, St. Louis; Ralph E. Hamersley, Louisville; and B. H. Schulte, Berkeley.

in 1973 as executive vice president-credit. It is doubtful whether any other man in the bank's history was subjected to a heavier work load than "Bob" was during 1972. In that year the bank relocated to Denver, acquired some $120 million in new commitments in five complicated new beet and cane sugar accounts and handled its billion dollar outstanding loan volume with a professional credit staff of only four. A commendable job was done, however, at great physical strain. The designation of Bob as executive vice president-credit was consistent with the scope of his responsibilities at the time.

Notwithstanding this broad delegation, there was mutual understanding that from time to time there would be an occasional loan with problems and risk of such magnitude that it would be treated as a "presidential loan." In all the years as a Farm Credit bank, there were five such loans. In 1974, there was only one and it was progressing to the point of regular servicing. A "presidential loan" took a goodly part of the President's time and sometimes for a while a majority of his time. For example, in one case the President and two other officers made weekly trips to a District Bank, seemingly for weeks on end, and also made a number of other trips in the interest of the satisfactory solution which was reached.

In 1975 in a reorganization Mr. Metzger became Senior Vice President of the bank.

The Loan Committee, 1965. It was the practice then to have all officers participate in loan committee actions. Seated, left to right: Fletcher B. Mills, B. F. Viehmann, Homer G. Smith, Dorwin Scott, Thomas E. Hall. Standing: A. N. Morrison, S. P. Hopkins, and R. W. Finn.

Gerald C. Drew

In 1967, the Central Bank engaged in another round of recruitment for its credit staff. It was seeking a competent credit officer, preferably one with experience in the canned and frozen fruit and vegetable industry. Jerry Drew was selected.

From Big Sandy, Montana, he held a master's degree from Montana State University. He had been a business analyst at the Spokane Bank for Cooperatives since 1960. He had served in the Army. Jerry was one of the four men on the credit staff in 1972. Early in 1975 he resigned to accept a position as assistant vice president of the Berkeley Bank for Cooperatives.

Donald M. Nettles

Mr. Nettles joined the bank as vice president in 1968. Previously, he was vice president and treasurer of the New Orleans Bank for Coopera-

The Loan Committee, 1966. Seated, left to right: Robert P. Simpson, Homer G. Smith, Fletcher B. Mills. Standing: A. N. Morrison, S. P. Hopkins, Thomas E. Hall, R. W. Finn and Hartwell A. Gilliard.

tives. A native of South Carolina, he received a bachelor's degree in business administration from the University of South Carolina. While with the bank, he completed the three-year course of the School of Banking of the South. He had served in the Army Signal Corps and had other broad experience as well: Special Agent-Intelligence, U.S. Treasury Department, public accounting and finance director, Jefferson Parish, Louisiana. He made a significant contribution to the Central Bank. In one serious problem participation loan situation, an unusual and fortuitous combination of circumstances and his prodigious and most capable efforts, working day and night over a long Thanksgiving weekend, proved to be of inestimable value to the banks, the borrower and many of the nation's farmers. He was effective in helping work out other credit problems. Mr. Nettles decided not to move to Denver and resigned in 1972.

The staff about 1970. (Perhaps the first time since 1961 that the number of staff members -thirteen- equalled the number of directors.) Front row, left to right: Mary Waldren, Secretary to the Treasurer; Patricia Heavener (now Mrs. Bassler), Secretary to the President; Robert L. Metzger; Homer G. Smith; Linda Bates; Mrs. Frances Fair, Accountant. Back row: R. W. Finn, D. N. Nettles, A. N. Morrison, Gerald C. Drew, S. P. Hopkins, H. A. Gilliard, and Thomas E. Hall.

William A. Terry, Sr.

A Texan with a bachelor's degree in agricultural economics from Texas A. & M. University, experience at Renner Research Foundation and Army service overseas, Bill joined the staff of the Houston Bank for Cooperatives in 1962 where he worked in the credit department and as assistant treasurer. He became assistant treasurer of the Central Bank in 1971.

Steve Staley

Mr. Staley was employed in 1972 and late in 1974 became assistant treasurer. Steve, a native of Billings, Montana, earned his bachelor's degree in accounting from the University of Missouri. While employed by the Central Bank he completed all of the tests necessary to qualify as a Certified Public Accountant and began work toward a master's degree with emphasis on finance at the University of Denver.

Treasurer's technical staff, 1972. As the relocation to Denver approached there had been a need to "shore up" the staff. Mr. Terry was employed as Assistant Treasurer in November 1971; Mr. Staley in 1972. Left to right: Frances Fair, R. W. Finn, Steve Staley, and William A. Terry.

Credit officers at the time of relocation to Denver, 1972.

Robert L. Metzger.

Daniel D. Williams.

Gerald C. Drew.

Hartwell A. Gilliard.

After the relocation to Denver, it was feasible to rapidly increase the credit staff to correct the serious understaffed situation which had developed. In succession numerous other credit officers joined the staff.

George H. Coulter

Mr. Coulter was born in North Dakota and reared on a farm in northeastern South Dakota. He served in the U.S. Army from 1953 to 1955. He graduated from Macalester College, St. Paul, Minnesota, in 1957 and earned a master's degree in agricultural economics from North Dakota State University in 1959. Mr. Coulter joined the staff of the St. Paul Bank for Cooperatives in 1959 as a business analyst and later joined the staff of the St. Louis Bank for Cooperatives. He held various positions in the Credit Department and ultimately served as vice president in charge of the Loan Department. From early 1970 to 1972, Mr. Coulter served as a vice president in the Commercial Loan Department of the Omaha National Bank, Omaha, Nebraska. He joined the Central Bank as a vice president.

Edward E. Crane

Ed was raised in Massachusetts and attended the University of Massachusetts. He worked with commercial banks in Arizona and Massachusetts for several years and served as an examiner for the Federal Reserve Bank of Boston from 1962 until 1965. For the following seven years, he served the Farm Credit Administration as an examiner, headquartered in the Spokane District. He joined the bank as an assistant vice president, and in 1976 became a vice president.

Gerald W. Emmer

Mr. Emmer was born and reared on a farm in east central Minnesota. He served with the U.S. Army Airborne Unit from 1952 to 1954. He earned a master's degree in agricultural economics from the University of Minnesota in 1959. He joined the staff of the St. Paul Bank for Cooperatives in 1959 as a business analyst. He held various positions there and from 1968 to 1971 served as vice president in charge of the bank's Credit Department. From November 1971 to February 1972 he was a special consultant to the Governor of the Farm Credit Administration with responsibility for coordinating the implementation of the Farm Credit Act

Credit officers employed after the relocation to Denver, 1972.

George H. Coulter, October, 1972.

Edward E. Crane, November, 1972.

Gerald W. Emmer, December, 1972.

Douglas D. Sims, February, 1974.

Robert O. Triplett, March, 1974.

of 1971. From February until December 1972, he was vice president of the Houston Bank for Cooperatives with responsibility for special loans and new business development. He then became a vice president of the Central Bank.

Douglas D. Sims

A native of Illinois, Mr. Sims graduated from the University of Illinois in 1968 with a bachelor's degree in agricultural economics. He joined the St. Louis Bank for Cooperatives in early 1969 and served in business analyst capacities in the Credit Department until 1972, when he joined the Federal Intermediate Credit Bank of St. Louis as assistant treasurer. Doug left his position of assistant vice president and assistant treasurer of the Federal Intermediate Credit Bank to join the Central Bank for Cooperatives as assistant vice president.

Robert O. Triplett

Coming from Rutherford, North Carolina, Mr. Triplett attended North Carolina State University where he earned a bachelor's degree in agricultural business-poultry in 1968. He then served as a business analyst with the Columbia Bank for Cooperatives. He had three years of active duty with the U.S. Air Force. He joined the credit staff of the Central Bank as assistant vice president, and subsequently began pursuit of a master's degree at the University of Denver.

With these additions, the credit staff, although still short on numbers for the overall job, was adequate for handling the credit situation of the day. It should be noted that each of the four vice presidents, including Mr. Metzger, in 1974 had headed the Credit Department of one of the District Banks for Cooperatives.

By 1974, there had truly been a major change in the bank. Its staff was larger than at any time since the years as a government bank. One area, however, had been somewhat neglected as the staff grew in size: that of internal administration.

Mrs. Juanita I. Reeves

A step toward correction was the employment in the fall of 1974 of Mrs. Reeves as assistant to the president.

Educated at Northwest Missouri State University and the University of Utah, she had several years of business experience in administration and accounting with major corporations, including commercial banking and manufacturing. In 1975, Mrs. Reeves became director of administrative services.

Some of the secretaries and the bookkeeper, 1974. Left to right: Darcy Brannigan, Secretary to Treasurer; Sharon Hutton, Secretary to President, Gail Hicks, Bookkeeper; Barbara Mullen, Secretary.

Assistant to the President, Juanita I. Reeves.

THE KEY ROLE OF THE CENTRAL BANK'S BOARD

The Board, as the governing body representative of the owners and having the full responsibility for the bank subject to the supervision of the Farm Credit Administration, naturally played an impressive part in the results attained. These included the credit service to farmer cooperatives, the financial strength and soundness of the bank and the building of good relations with District Banks.

In the general Farm Credit tradition, Board members are not salaried and serve strictly on a part-time basis. In a real sense they speak for farmers and ranchers, the ultimate owners of the bank through their local and regional cooperatives which borrow from the District Banks for Cooperatives, which in turn own the Central Bank. This means of maintaining the grass roots touch is an important source of strength for the bank.

A most significant decision made in January 1956, when the Board took control, was that it would continue to hold regular meetings on a quarterly basis. Special meetings, held as needed, tend to average about two a year, including a traditional special meeting incident to the annual stockholder's conference.

The decision to hold a number of regularly scheduled meetings in the various Farm Credit Districts permitted the Board to meet with District Directors and officers and usually with representatives of participation borrowers. It also enabled the Board to observe the agriculture of the different areas and cooperative facilities and occasionally export operations and port facilities. Wives were encouraged to accompany participants, although at their personal expense.

In the late 1960s a Director observed that the better part of his three-year term was required to gain an understanding of the role of the Central Bank and its plan of operation. At the Board's request, the staff initiated annual orientation meetings for new Directors. These meetings were well received.

Board of Directors, 1971. New Directors: seated, at left, Ben Swigart, Oklahoma; third from right, Kenneth M. Noble, New York; at right, Melvin A. Ensley, Washington; standing, at left, William Kenneth Miller, Indiana; third from left, Howard F. Robinson; fourth from left, William T. Steele, Virginia; fifth from left, Darrell D. Moseson; sixth from left, Hilmer E. Albrecht, Illinois.

Group tour at Superior, Wisconsin, 1973.

BOARD CHAIRMEN: 1956 to 1976

A basic concept was followed. The Chairman of the Board was the policy head of the bank, recognizing of course that policies could be established only by the Board acting as a Board. The President, as chief executive officer, operated the bank.

F. R. Wilcox, Los Angeles, California
Director 1952-1966
Chairman 1956-1964

A student of marketing, Mr. Wilcox after varied experience became the General Manager of Sunkist headquartered in Los Angeles. He was named as a Director of the Central Bank in 1952. In the fifteen years of his service the bank weathered many a storm. This period included the bank's last four years as a government bank and the first eleven years as a Farm Credit bank. In his nine years as Chairman he made notable contributions to the solution of many problems of policy and relations. These were the most difficult years in the bank's history because to a degree the bank was not wanted by its potential owners.

Mr. Wilcox was very active in the affairs of the National Council of Farmer Cooperatives and served as its president. Following his retirement from Sunkist in 1965 he remained active. He died in 1972.

K. N. Probasco, Columbus Ohio
Director 1957-1968
Chairman 1965-1966

With a bachelor's degree from Ohio State University, Mr. Probasco joined the staff of Landmark, Inc. (formerly Farm Bureau Cooperative Association, Inc.) in Columbus, Ohio. He became executive vice president and general manager in 1955. He was a member and chairman of the Board of the Farm Credit Banks of Louisville.

He was elected as a member of the initial seven-man Board of the"new" Central Bank and served twelve years. He was one of the Directors who bore the brunt, particularly at St. Louis in 1956 and Omaha in 1957, of considerable hostility to the Central Bank. He contributed greatly to the solutions of the problems. He was Board Chairman at the time of a most successful National Farm Credit Directors Conference hosted by the Central Bank. He served on the Federal Farm Credit Board and became Chairman while this book was in process. He is a Director of the National Council of Farmer Cooperatives and a Certified Public Accountant. He was a member of the Board of Trustees of the American Institute of Cooperation.

Walter W. Peterson, Chappell, Nebraska
Director 1962-1967
Chairman 1967

Walter Peterson is a son of Henry C. Peterson, one of the "great American cooperators." Walter served as manager of the Farmers Elevator Co. at Chappell, Nebraska for thirty-two years. He also served as secretary of Westcentral Cooperative Grain Co. He was an organizer and the president of FAR-MAR-CO, which resulted from the merger of four regional grain cooperatives in 1968. He is a member and past chairman of the Board of the Farm Credit Banks of Omaha. He and his wife Idris co-chaired the committee on arrangements for the National Farm Credit Directors Conference hosted by the Central Bank. There is a special characteristic and ability for which he is noted—that of calming troubled waters and developing sound, amicable, solutions. This ability served the Central Bank well. When he became a Central Bank Director the new limit on tenure to two consecutive full three-year terms was in effect. (This provision of the Farm Credit Act of 1960 was eliminated by the Farm Credit Act of 1971.)

James H. Dean, Hutchinson, Kansas
Director 1955-1968
Chairman 1968

Mr. Dean's career was dedicated to serving farmers through their grain cooperatives. Starting in a local elevator in Kansas he became the general manager of Farmers Cooperative Commission Co., Hutchinson, Kansas. He played a key role in the merger negotiations which resulted in FAR-MAR-CO and he was elected as its general manager, a post he held until his retirement in 1973. Mr. Dean's fourteen years as a member of the Central Bank Board embraced the last of its government years and the entire period of transition to the beginnings of the "modern" Central Bank in 1968. In one highly controversial and critical participation loan

Board chairmen, 1956-1976.

F. R. Wilcox, 1956-1964.

K. N. Probasco, 1965-1966.

Walter W. Peterson, 1967.

James H. Dean, 1968.

Guido Schroeder, 1969-1970.

John T. Lesley, 1971.

Glen R. Harris, 1972-1973.

Melvin A. Ensley, 1974-1975.

Wilmer Smith, 1976.

situation he firmly supported the concept of holding management responsible for handling the situation. This led to a Board decision which proved to be appropriate and set an important precedent. He was named to a six-year term as a member of the Federal Farm Credit Board and was its vice-chairman. He was very active in the National Federation of Grain Cooperatives and was its president. He was a member of the Board of Trustees of the American Institute of Cooperation.

Guido Schroeder, West Bend, Wisconsin
Director 1965-1970
Chairman 1969-1970

Mr. Schroeder is a dairy farmer. He was active in dairy cooperatives and in production credit, and was president of the Juneau, Wisconsin Production Credit Association and a member of the Production Credit National Advisory Committee at the time of the Farm Credit Act of 1953. He was a member and chairman of the Board of the Farm Credit Banks of St. Paul.

Mr. Schroeder was a "scrapper" for farmers. He was one of the many leaders dedicated to providing a dependable source of credit for agriculture and to have it farmer-owned and controlled. His two years as Chairman occurred in the period of transition to adjust to the key actions in 1968.

John T. Lesley, Tampa, Florida
Director 1963-1971
Chairman 1971

Mr. Lesley was an effective leader in the cooperative citrus industry in Florida. He was chairman of the Board of the Farm Credit Banks of Columbia. He had the responsibilities for many years as general manager of Seald Sweet. High on the list of his many valuable contributions to the Central Bank during his nine years of service was his suggestion during the 1968 annual stockholder's conference that there should be a capital committee of the Board. The activation of the committee was a key development. It brought the Board for the first time to a position of real influence in this phase of its responsibilities, coincident with the adoption of the base capital plan. Mr. Lesley was very active in the affairs of the National Council of Farmer Cooperatives and served as a director.

Glen R. Harris, Richvale, California
Director 1967-1975
Chairman 1972-1973

Mr. Harris is a farmer whose major crop is rice. He was vice chairman of the Board of the Rice Growers Association of California. He was very active in production credit in both the Chico and Colusa Associations, serving as president of the Chico Association for twenty-five years from its organization in 1933.

He was a member of the Production Credit National Advisory Committee at the time of the 1953 act, and later became a member of the Federal Farm Credit Board and served as its chairman.

His depth of farm credit experience was invaluable to the Central Bank. Among his many key suggestions were to propose in January 1969 that the bank push at that time for a relaxation of the Farm Credit Administration's prior approval procedures, and to recommend in 1973 that the Board take action to demonstrate that it held the firm view that the time had come when a Banks for Cooperatives bond issue each month was urgently needed.

He became an enthusiastic supporter of the need of the bank to build a more adequate credit staff to better serve the District Banks. He was active for years in the affairs of the National Council of Farmer Cooperatives, serving as a director representing his cooperative. Mr. Harris was vice chairman of the Commission on Agricultural Credit which functioned in 1969 and 1970.

Melvin A. Ensley, Colfax, Washington
Director 1968-present
Chairman 1974-1975

Mr. Ensley raises wheat and peas on the steep hills of the Palouse area in eastern Washington. Each harvest must bring exhilaration and pride, but with some risk to life itself. He came to the Central Bank Board just as major changes were occurring in escalating loan volume and in a new prestige and opportunities for the bank. He is a member and past chairman of the Board of the Farm Credit Banks of Spokane.

He served as chairman in 1973 of the Farm Credit System Management Development Study Committee. The work of that committee had a profound effect on the Central Bank. For years it had been Banks for

Cooperatives System policy to keep the number of personnel at rock bottom levels. The concept finally prevailed that this was basically unsound and that the future of the system in its credit service and the avoidance of serious losses was dependent on building and training staff adequate to the new and prospective situation.

Wilmer Smith, Wilson, Texas
Director 1957-1965, 1972-present
Chairman 1976

Mr. Wilmer Smith was vice chairman in 1974 and the senior active director in years of service. In 1957, he had been appointed as a member of the first seven-man Board of the "new" Central Bank. He continued as a Director through 1965 including the period of transition to the thirteen-man Board in 1961. In 1972, he became the only Director to have a second tour of duty on the Board. Thus he had served twelve years through 1974. As this book was being completed in 1976 he was in his fourteenth year and was Chairman. A cotton grower, he used to say that when the third tractor was in use, he was driving it. He had been a leader of cooperatives in his area. He had been active in the cotton industry nationally. He was chairman of the National Advisory Committee to the Banks for Cooperatives during the critical period of the enactment of the Farm Credit Act of 1955. He was a personal confidant to the author and a pillar of strength during the late 1950s, when the problems of the bank were critical. He has been a member of the Board of the Farm Credit Banks of Houston since 1965, and is a former member of the Board of Directors of Texas Tech University.

SUPERVISION AND EXAMINATION BY THE FARM CREDIT ADMINISTRATION

Supervision by the Farm Credit Administration was essential and constructive. Its leadership in obtaining needed legislation and maintaining good relations in Washington was outstanding. By regulating and coordinating the sytem, the Farm Credit Administration helped mold it and contributed to its functioning and was instrumental in the sale of the system's bonds.

The Central Bank is examined each year by Farm Credit Administration examiners, and the bank's published annual financial statements include the opinion of the Farm Credit Administration's Examination Division.

During this period the Governors guided the bank's course. C. R. "Cap" Arnold served as Governor in 1953 in the critical period of transition following the reestablishment of the Farm Credit Administration as an independent agency. He led in the development of the Production Credit System and was an advocate of farmer ownership and increased farmer control. R. B. Tootell served as Governor from 1954 to 1969—the years of implementation of the Farm Credit Act of 1953. During this period a number of Farm Credit acts became law, including that of 1954, under which the thirteen banks could issue consolidated bonds, that of 1955, under which the Central Bank became a Farm Credit bank run by its own officers as elected by its Board, and that of 1960, under which the seven-man Board was replaced by a thirteen-man Board with provision ultimately for one member to be elected by each of the District Boards. During his tenure all of the banks and associations of the entire Farm Credit System attained complete farmer ownership.

From 1956 on, Tootell was supported in the supervisory role by R. C. Mahone and Glenn E. Heitz, who served successively as Deputy Governor and Director of the Cooperative Bank Service.

From 1969 to 1974, the Governor's position was held by E. A. Jaenke. During his administration, the Central Bank's role as a bank of participation was expanded by changing the lending limit policy. In addition there was significant relaxation in the administration's prior loan approval requirements. Funding options were increased as a result of the Farm Credit Act of 1971, which also permitted the relocation of the bank from Washington, D.C. to Denver. In addition, it relaxed "voting media" requirements on Rural Electric Association loans. There was a notable relaxation in the prior tight controls over maximum salary levels. The supporting role as Director of the Cooperative Bank Service was carried by Donald E. Roark from 1970 to 1972 when the office was eliminated through organizational change. Malcolm W. Harding, who had a lifelong career in farm credit, assumed the office of Governor in November 1974.

The Farm Credit Administration's Deputy Governors who served as Directors of the Cooperative Bank Service were in an especially close relationship to all of the Banks for Cooperatives.

Farm Credit Administration Deputy Governors and Directors of the Cooperative Bank Service, 1956-1972.

R. C. Mahone, 1957-1959.

Glenn E. Heitz, 1959-1969.

Donald E. Roark, 1970-1972.

*Malcom Harding, Governor,
Farm Credit Administration, 1974 to present.*

OTHER SERVICES PROVIDED BY THE FARM CREDIT ADMINISTRATION

Farm Credit Administration officials and staff, in addition to their role in supervision, were most helpful to the bank in many support functions, which the bank gradually assumed as its own. However, the Farm Credit Administration, incident to its role in supervision, continued to help the Central Bank in a number of ways. The services of the administration are deeply appreciated.

5

The Central Bank in 1974
A Period of Transition

The bank's basic function is to supplement and expand the role of its twelve District Bank owners to permit them to better serve farmer cooperatives and their farmer members. This is primarily accomplished through purchasing, in loans made by the District Banks, amounts usually in excess of the lending limits on a single credit risk. The relationship is contractual through a participation agreement. The objective is to spread the risk and thus permit the system to provide extensive credit service on a sound basis.

Chart 3 illustrates the bank's essential business of participating loans. The top line indicates that during a two-year period of major loan activity there were nine increases and one decrease in the line of credit to the cooperative. The second line shows that the outstanding balance of the loan closely approached the total available line of credit—except during two periods of heavy seasonal loan liquidation. The third line indicates that in this particular loan illustration most of the outstanding loans (and thus the loan activity) were carried by the Central Bank.

The extreme example of Chart 3 is provided to illustrate the nature of the Central Bank's participation role in a considerable number of instances. There were many other participation loans where the Central Bank's role was less significant.

Chart 3
Example of Financing a Cooperative Through Participation
Two-Year Period, July 1, 1972 to June 30, 1974

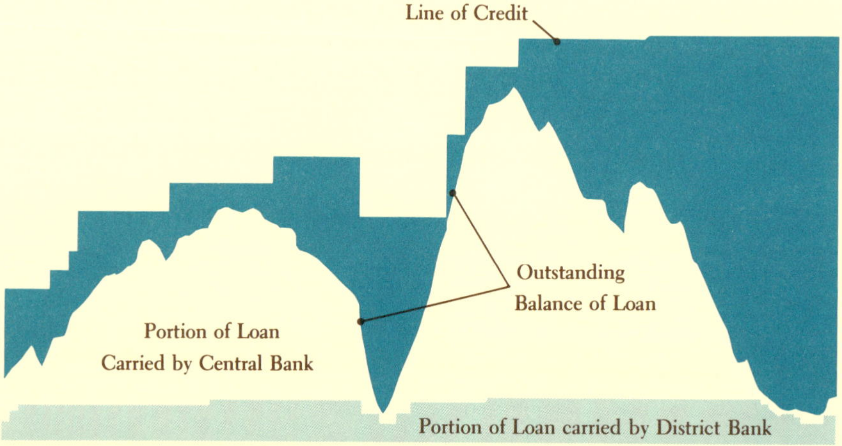

Participation by the Central Bank in loans of a District Bank means that the Central Bank provides a portion of the money loaned (usually above the lending limit of the District Bank) and shares in (a) the interest income, (b) the risk of loss, and thus (c) the credit decisions. Patronage refunds resulting from the total net savings of the Central Bank are distributed to the District Banks for Cooperatives based on the interest paid to the Central Bank on participations. The District Bank services loans in which the Central Bank participates; however, the Central Bank considers itself as a full partner with the District Bank in the financing.

GREAT INCREASE IN LOANS

Although loan activity and volume growth occurred steadily, a major growth spurt began in January 1973 as the Commodity Credit Corporation's operations were significantly contracted. This was the result of many factors, including the large reduction of its inventories as the nation's surpluses were utilized and a market price structure of staple farm commodities much higher than Commodity Credit Corporation loan levels, which reduced loans to farmers from that organization. Also, there were major increases in Central Bank loans late in 1974, notably to farm supply and fruit and vegetable cooperatives. The Banks for Cooperatives System had been able to meet effectively the challenge presented, and had been able to carry its share of the resulting major increase in the financing of farmer cooperatives.

SIZE OF LOANS

Loans were large because many of the participation borrowers grew in size as their services to their farmer members in marketing farm products and in providing essential farm supplies increased and as inflation caused increases in price levels. In general, a loan was not offered to the Central Bank until its amount exceeded the lending limits of the District Bank. By December 31, 1974, the average size of the Central Bank's participation loan commitments, including both the disbursed and undisbursed portions, was as follows:

Total Central Bank commitments to participate in loans to farmer cooperatives:	$3,125 million
Number of cooperatives: 103	
Average size of Central Bank commitments:	30.3 million

Central Bank participation loans, although to a relatively small number of cooperatives, affected a majority of the nation's farmers and ranchers. The larger loans usually were to regional cooperatives or federations of regionals, and through them had an impact on a large number of local cooperatives and their farmer members.

BASIS FOR LARGE LOANS

Large loans, so greatly needed by farmer cooperatives to serve their farmer members, could be made because lending limits on Central Bank participation loans were based on the capitalization of the entire system. The adjusted system capitalization was $391.8 million on June 30, 1974.

SYSTEM CAPITAL "POOLED"

There was sound rationale for using adjusted system net worth as a base for the lending limits on participation loans.

The thirteen Banks for Cooperatives were jointly and severally responsible for their system's bonds. Also, by contractual arrangements the Central Bank Board had an unlimited call on the capital of the twelve District Banks, subject only to the approval of the Farm Credit Administration. There was no practical possibility of abuse of this authority because of the democratic way the system operated. At the other extreme, it was a function of the Central Bank to provide funds to any of the District Banks which could not reasonably obtain funds from any other source. Thus it is significant that, while each of the thirteen banks operated autonomously under Farm Credit Administration supervision, in effect the capital of the entire system was pooled in case of need.

LENDING LIMITS

The preceding discussion leads directly to the matter of lending limits on a single credit risk. The 1974-1975 lending limits for each of the thirteen banks, as established by the Farm Credit Administration, are shown in Table 9. The lending limits were critically important to the

Table 9
Lending Limits of the Banks for Cooperatives
Fiscal Year July 1, 1974 to June 30, 1975[a]

Bank	Total Net Worth 6/30/74	Limit on Term Loans (25% of Net Worth)	Limit on Seasonal Loans Other than Commodity (35% of Net Worth)	Limit on Seasonal Commodity Loans (50% of Net Worth)
		millions		
Springfield	$ 16.5	$ 4.1	$ 5.8	$ 8.2
Baltimore	15.1	3.8	5.3	7.5
Columbia	31.2	7.8	10.9	15.6
Louisville	28.8	7.2	10.1	14.4
New Orleans	23.6	5.9	8.3	11.8
St. Louis	41.4	10.3	14.5	20.7
St. Paul	48.8	12.1	17.1	24.4
Omaha	25.8	6.4	9.0	12.9
Wichita	40.4	10.1	14.1	20.2
Houston	27.4	6.8	9.6	13.7
Berkeley	35.5	8.9	12.4	17.8
Spokane	25.0[b]	6.2	8.7	12.5
Banks for Cooperatives System	391.8[c]	97.9	137.1	195.9

[a] Central Bank limit on participation loans purchased could not exceed the amount established for the Banks for Cooperatives System less amounts held by District Banks. Central Bank direct loans to cooperatives (of which there were none in 1974), exclusive of participations sold, could not exceed the lending limit percentages prescribed for District Banks based on the Central Bank's net worth of $150.4 million. Classifications (term, seasonal-other and commodity) and the application of lending limits are explained in Chapter VI.

[b] The net worth of the Spokane Bank is as of July 31, 1974.

[c] The system total includes $36.3 million of net worth of the Central Bank not represented by stock owned by or equities allocated to District Banks.

Central Bank. It desired that the lending District Bank assume as large a portion of the total risk of a loan as was determined to be sound in light of the District Bank's capital structure and appropriate risk exposure. On the other hand, the Central Bank's basic function was to provide the portion of the loans which exceeded District Banks' lending limits.

SCOPE OF OPERATIONS: TURNOVER OF LOAN FUNDS

In 1973 and 1974, the Central Bank experienced a level of calls for loan funds never before approached by any of the Farm Credit banks. This resulted from the bank's long-established role as a key provider of seasonal loan funds for most of the nation's larger farmer cooperatives, the unprecedented financing of inventories of grain, cotton, and other commodities, and the great increase in the seasonal need for loan funds as farm supply cooperatives financed the large and higher priced inventories of fertilizer and petroleum products and the related accounts receivable before payment was made by farmers.

During this time the Central Bank's outstanding participation loans increased $442 million in the three-month period from October through December 1974, and the bank's outstanding seasonal participation loans increased 91 percent in the year ended December 31, 1974, at that date comprising 73.5 percent of total outstanding Central Bank participation loans (see Table 10).

Table 10
The Central Bank's Participation Loans

Loan Type	Amount Outstanding as of December 31		
	1974	1973	Increase
		millions	
Seasonal	$1,102	$577	91%
Term (maturing in over a year)	398	349	14%
Total	1,500	926	62%
Seasonal loans as a percent of total	73.5%	62.3%	

As an illustration of turnover, loan advances on participation loans for the calendar year 1974 totalled $4.4 billion as compared to the average amount outstanding of $1.1 billion. The same funds may be used over and over as the harvest moves from south to north and as the need for funds to finance various commodities and cooperative categories occurs at different times.

Chart 4 shows the peak and low points of outstanding Central Bank participation loans by category for the calendar year 1974. It will be noted that participation loans to cooperatives classified as "farm supplies" moved from a low point of $242.2 million at the end of June to $544.6 million at the end of December; loans to cooperatives classified as "grain" dropped seasonally from $287.3 million in January to $40 million in May.

The seasonal swings in the Central Bank's participation loan business by category are shown in Chart 5, which covers the three years of 1972 through 1974.

Although seven classifications are used in the two charts—farm supplies, grain, fruits and vegetables, dairy, fertilizer, cotton and all others—the entire loan to a cooperative was included in a single classification. The bank maintained no records which would permit any other approach. A farm supply cooperative might have a grain department, fertilizer operation or marketing operation. However, the entire loan was classified as farm supplies. Accordingly, the financing of grain, fertilizer and marketing operations was more extensive than the charts would indicate. Similarly, even though a dairy cooperative might have a farm supply operation the entire loan was classified as dairy, again leading to unavoidable distortion.

FUNDING

In 1973 and 1974 the Central Bank had unprecedented fluctuations in the need for borrowed funds. These resulted from the extreme and unpredictable variations in loans.

Chart 6 shows that the same influences which caused the fluctuations in outstanding participation loans of the Central Bank (bottom line) also affected the twelve District Banks for Cooperatives and thus the entire Banks for Cooperatives System (top line). However, the effect on the Central Bank in handling most of the fluctuations in the larger loans to farmer cooperatives was greater than its share of the total loan volume of the thirteen banks in the system.

The bank adapted its funding patterns over the years to meet changing situations with the key objective of obtaining loanable funds at the lowest feasible cost but with assurance that needed funds would be available. This adaptation is discussed in considerable detail in Chapter 7.

Chart 4
Peak and Low Points—Outstanding Participation Loans by Category, Month-End Account Balances, Calendar Year, 1974

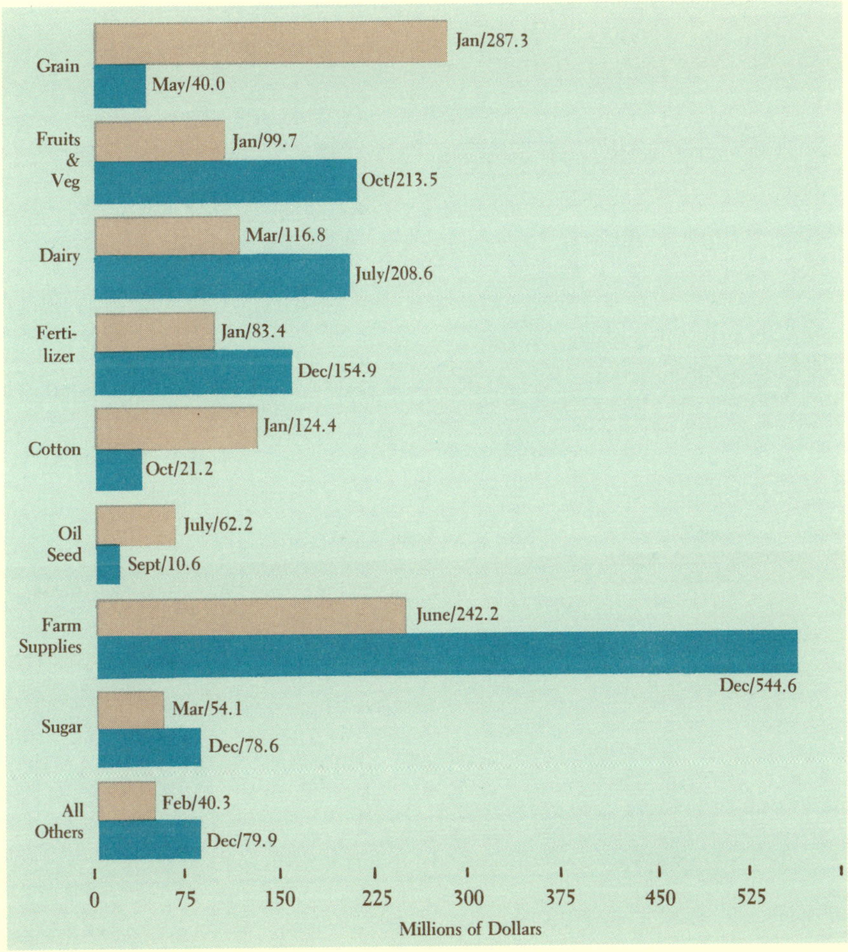

Chart 5
Composition of Loans by Category for 1972, 1973, and 1974

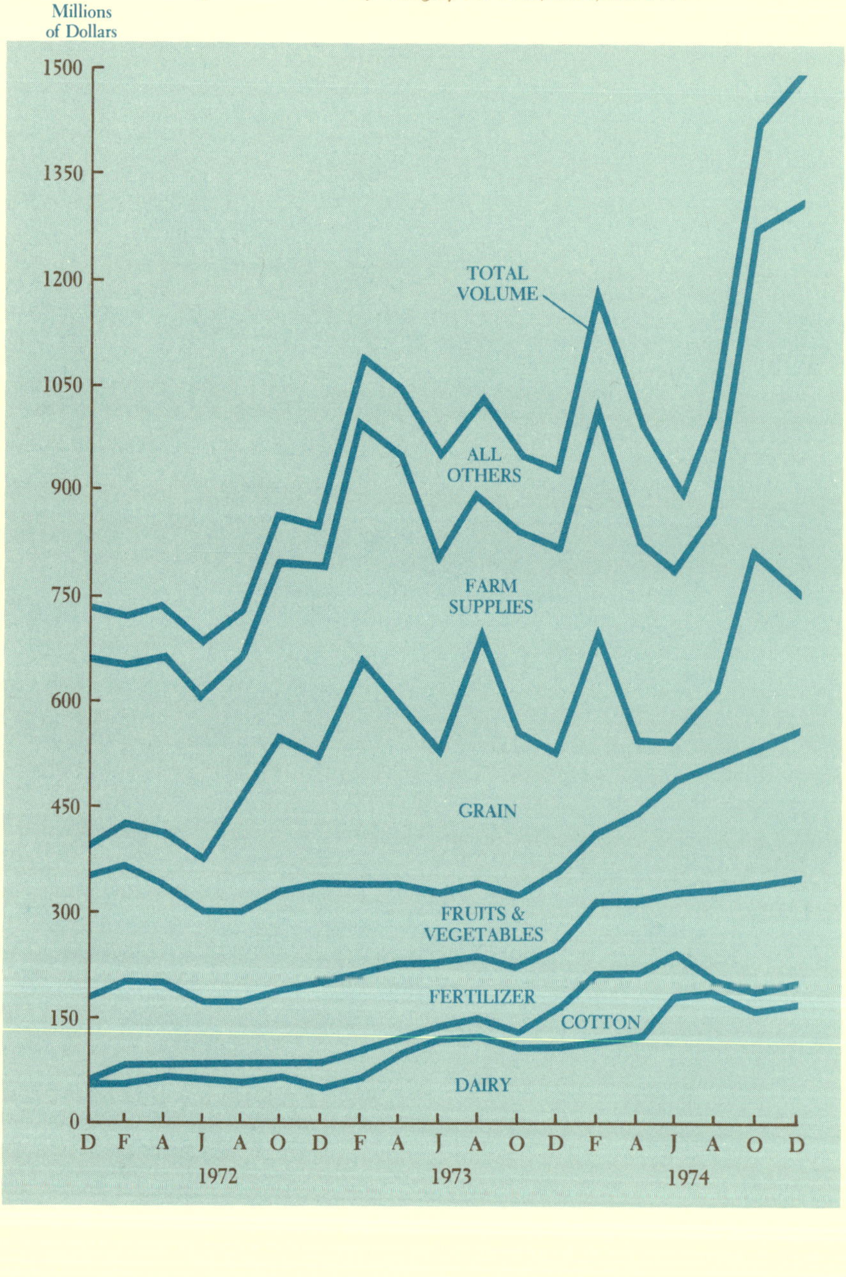

Chart 6
Banks for Cooperatives System

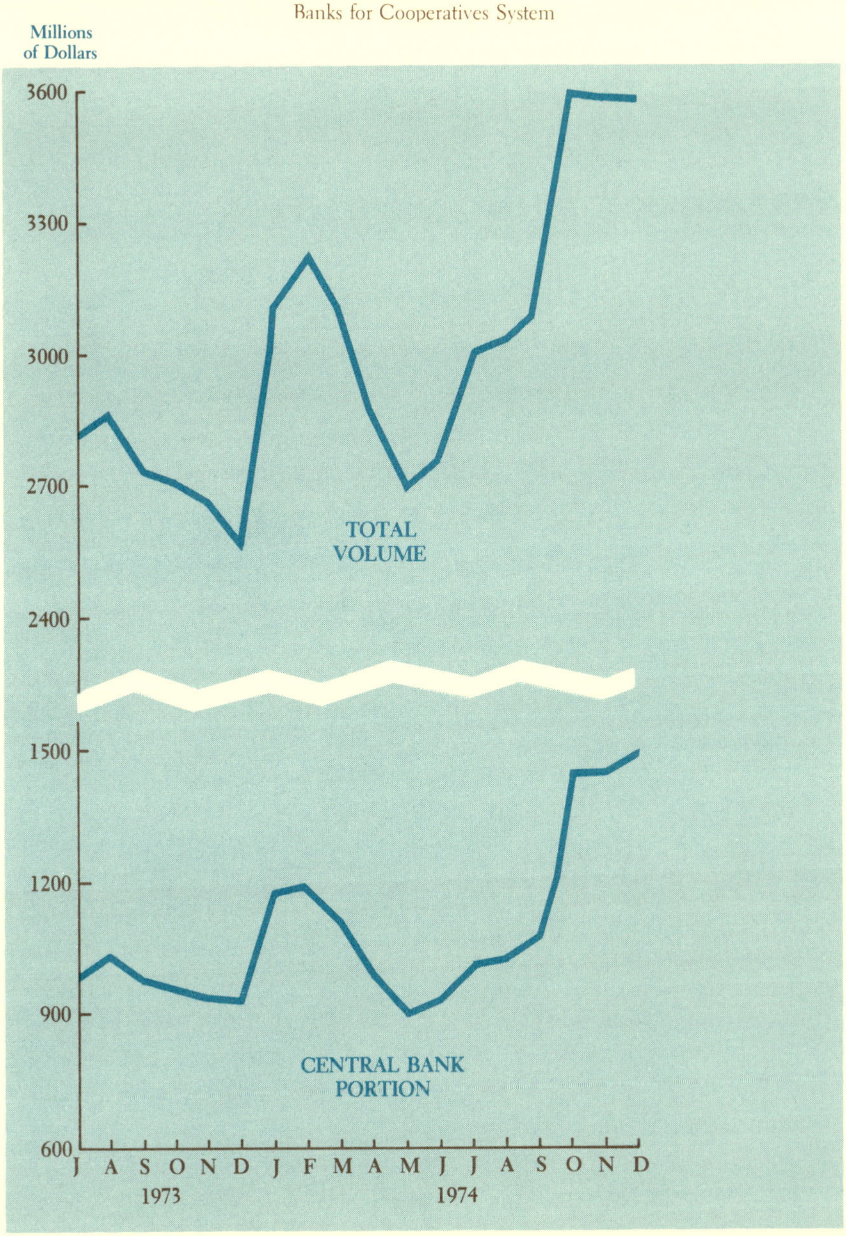

STAFF

Because it served as a bank of participation, and in a sense a "banker's bank," the bank was able to operate with a small but highly skilled staff.

Under this plan, loan applications from farmer cooperatives originated at the District Bank level, where the basic credit analysis and loan servicing was carried out. The Central Bank, however, insisted that it be a full partner in the financing, and its staff worked with the District Banks, and as appropriate with their borrowers (jointly with the District Banks), to ensure that result.

The staff organization of the bank in effect in February 1974 is shown in Chart 7.

The staff of officers in the Credit Department, which had been reduced to four in the fall of 1972 partially because of the relocation from Washington, D.C. to Denver, had been increased to nine by 1974 with the employment of two additional vice presidents and three assistant vice presidents. Staffing had proceeded as rapidly as was feasible, particularly in view of the change in presidents effective August 1, 1974. Still needed were a general counsel, an agricultural economist, an additional vice president and assistant vice president in the Credit Department, and a computer specialist and financial analyst in the Treasurer's Department.

It was obvious that good results could be attained only through excellent working relationships with the District Banks. The Central Bank staff needed to be attuned to and considerate of District Banks' views because of their closer working relationship with a borrower and their more intimate knowledge of the local situation. The District Banks, in turn, needed to give recognition to the responsibilities of the Central Bank staff under a Board on behalf of the entire Banks for Cooperatives System, and be mindful of the broader, overall knowledge which the Central Bank staff should have by virtue of its nationwide experience and knowledge of the financing of most of the nation's large farmer cooperatives, as well as its extensive experience in the handling of large problem loans.

This operating plan required special staff characteristics and qualifications, particularly in view of the size, complexity and risks often inherent in many of the participation loans.

The financing staff especially had major responsibilities which it met smoothly.

Chart 7
Central Bank for Cooperatives, Denver, Colorado

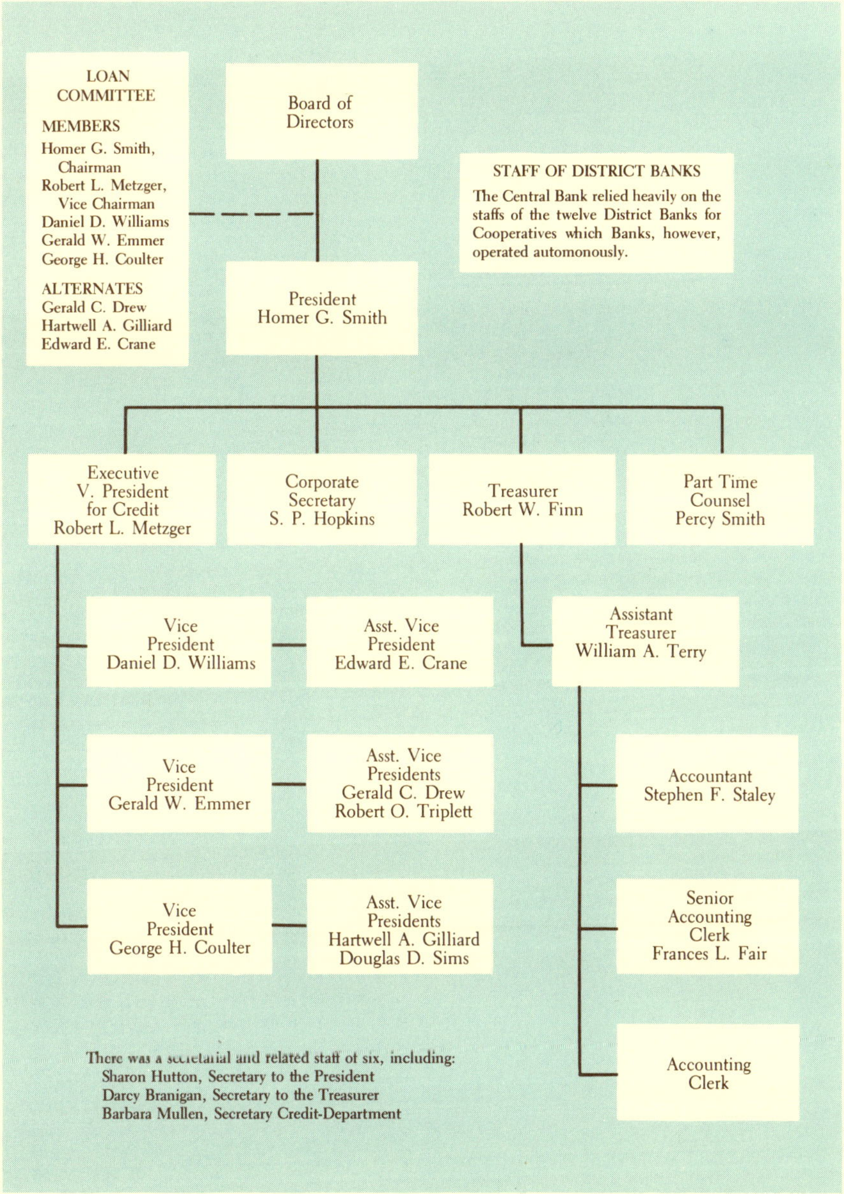

Senior officers under the president, February 1974.

Robert L. Metzger,
Executive Vice President-Credit.

Daniel D. Williams, Vice President.

Gerald E. Emmer, Vice President.

George H. Coulter, Vice President.

S. P. Hopkins, Corporate Secretary.

Robert W. Finn, Treasurer.

Percy Smith, Part Time Counsel.

NET SAVINGS

Net savings for the year ended June 30, 1974, amounted to $15.8 million, representing a return of 11.25 percent on average net worth or 13.34 percent if computed before the provision of $2.9 million for bad debts.

The patronage refund to District Banks for Cooperatives averaged 17.6 percent of the interest received by the Central Bank on participation loans. This refund was, in effect, paid to the District Banks in cash.

The interest income of the Central Bank on participation loans has been based upon the interest rates set by the District Banks, which at times have been much lower than the prime rate of commercial banks. It should be pointed out that an increase of 0.1 percent in 1974 would have added $1 million to the Central Bank's income. An increase of 1 percent in 1974 would have added $10 million and increased the return on net worth to 20.47 percent before provision for loan losses. Comments on pricing policy are included in Chapter 12.

Net savings were distributed to the District Banks based upon interest paid to the Central Bank on participation loans. The distribution worked this way: if the average rate of interest received by the Central Bank on all participation loans was 6 percent and all District Banks had sold the Central Bank an equal amount of participations, a bank which was charging 6¼ percent would receive an added distribution equal to the dollar value of the ¼ percent and a bank charging 5¾ percent would be docked the same dollar amount. Thus, in theory, each District Bank received its patronage based on its contribution to Central Bank income. That plan, in effect since 1972, has been more equitable than the plan previously used on which patronage was based on a single percentage (applicable uniformly to all District Banks) of the interest received by the Central Bank on participation loans, regardless of variations between District Banks in their levels of interest rates.

FINANCIAL CONDITION

Figures on financial condition and operations are included in the statements in Chapter 4.

OWNERSHIP

Table 11 shows the amount of capital owned by each of the twelve District Banks, plus their interest in the allocated surplus. Also shown is the Central Bank's unallocated surplus, all as of June 30, 1974, the close of the 1973-1974 fiscal year.

Table 11
Ownership of the Central Bank
June 30, 1974

District Bank	Total of Capital Stock Owned and Equity in Allocated Surplus
	millions
Springfield	$ 9.9
Baltimore	5.4
Columbia	11.7
Louisville	6.9
New Orleans	10.4
St. Louis	7.8
St. Paul	15.0
Omaha	2.0
Wichita	15.1
Houston	8.2
Berkeley	13.4
Spokane	8.3
Total District Bank allocated equities	$114.1
Surplus reserved, unallocated	29.7*a*
Surplus other, unallocated	6.6*b*
Total net worth	$150.4

a This item arose from the bank's retained net earnings in its government years. The Farm Credit Acts of 1955 and 1971 prohibit the distribution of this surplus as patronage refunds.

b This item arose from two sources: (1) The discount of $1.3 million allowed by the government on the final retirement in 1968 ahead of statutory requirements of the remaining capital stock owned by the government pursuant to special legislation and (2) the transfer to surplus of the $5.3 million reserve for bad debts created in the government years to conform with an Internal Revenue ruling that for tax purposes it was in fact surplus. These additions were offset by a minor subsequent reduction.

CONTROL

Twelve members of the Board of Directors are elected, one each by the District Farm Credit Board in the twelve Farm Credit districts. A thirteenth is appointed by the Governor of the Farm Credit Administration with the concurrence of the Federal Farm Credit Board.

The Board's primary responsibilities have included determination of policy, selection of hired management, approval of the budget, decisions as to distribution of net savings, and a continuous review of operations through reports of management, review of participation loans, and the study of reports of examination.

A PERIOD OF TRANSITION

The period of 1968 to 1974 saw momentous changes, particularly in 1973 and 1974. Long-standing impediments, particularly permissible salary levels and bank location, which had made top staff recruitment most difficult, had been alleviated, and progress had been made in lifting a long-standing burden resulting from the Farm Credit Administration's insistence on prior approval of practically all Central Bank participation loans. This policy, together with the procedures followed (under which a District Bank usually requested action on a loan by both the Central Bank and the Farm Credit Administration on the basis of its concurrent requests), had placed the Central Bank in an unusual, difficult and at times badly misunderstood position.

THE NEW PRESIDENT

In February 1974, following a thorough executive search, the Board of Directors announced the election of Bernard H. Schulte as President effective August 1, 1974. He was to succeed Homer G. Smith, who had served as the bank's chief executive officer since 1954 and as President since 1956, when that office was established.

Mr. Schulte was then president of the Berkeley Bank for Cooperatives in Berkeley, California.

Son of a fruit grower and agricultural leader in the Monterey County area of California, Schulte earned a master's degree in agricultural economics from the University of California. He served for four and a half years in the U.S. Army in World War II and was discharged with the rank of major.

Having served on several national committees in the Farm Credit System, he was chairman in 1974 of the Finance Committee of the Banks for Cooperatives, which is charged with setting maturities and the pricing of Banks for Cooperatives' bond issues. During 1973 he had served as Chairman of the President's Committee of the Farm Credit Banks of Berkeley.

The new President, Bernard H. Schulte.

Board of Directors, 1974.

District 12–Spokane: Melvin A. Ensley–Chairman, Colfax, Washington, Grain and Livestock Farmer.

District 10–Houston: Wilmer Smith–Vice Chairman, Wilson, Texas, Cotton Grower.

District 1–Springfield: Henry W. Bibus, Wrightstown, New Jersey, Fruit and Vegetable Producer.

District 2–Baltimore: John W. Stone, Spencer, West Virginia, Livestock Farmer.

District 3–Columbia: A. J. Haynes, Todd, North Carolina, Retired President and General Manager, FCX Inc.

District 4–Louisville: Wm. Kenneth Miller, Indianapolis, Indiana, Retired Assistant General Manager, Indiana Farm Bureau Cooperative.

District 5–New Orleans: Joseph A. Kyser, Greensboro, Alabama, Farmer–Catfish and Livestock.

District 6–St. Louis: Hilmer E. Albrecht, Sparta, Illinois, General Manager, Randolph Service Company.

District 7–St. Paul: Darrell D. Moseson, South St. Paul, Minnesota, Senior Vice President, Finance, CENEX.

District 8–Omaha: Fred J. Ludwig, Laurens, Iowa, Grain Farmer.

District 9–Wichita: James R. Isleib, Shawnee Mission, Kansas, Retired executive, Former Land Bank Commissioner.

District 11–Berkeley: Glen R. Harris, Richvale, California, Rice Grower.

Director at Large: Howard F. Robinson, Greensboro, North Carolina, Director, Research Administration and Professor of Agricultural Economics, North Carolina A & T State University.

Four new Board members.

*Mark L. Keith,
Columbus, Ohio, 1975.*

*William D. Lakey,
Sayre, Oklahoma, 1975.*

*Lee R. Kolmer,
Ames, Iowa, 1976.*

*Howard A. Wuertz,
Coolidge, Arizona, 1976.*

6

The Great Adventures in Credit Over the Years

GENERAL FINANCING

Work in the Central Bank has provided the opportunity to participate in the financing of most of the nation's large farmer cooperatives. Some $23.6 billion in loan advances had been made through 1974, comprised of $2.1 billion in loans made by Central Bank directly to farmer cooperatives in its early years and $21.5 billion in participations purchased in loans of District Banks. The loans have assisted in the financing of facilities and operations which have contributed greatly to the income and well-being of the nation's farmers. The loans have contributed to the production, handling and processing of food and fiber for the nation and the world and the U.S. balance of payments. Constructive loans were made and collected under a courageous lending policy, and the course of the Central Bank's development has been exciting as the bank and District Banks worked cooperatively with borrowers to agree on a basis on which major and at times bold ventures could be financed.

Grain Financing

Many of today's major grain cooperatives were originally financed through the revolving fund and the Central Bank, or through District Banks with Central Bank participation. Loans were made for both storage and export facilities and also for grain processing plants.

Seasonal financing of grain has been the bank's most volatile lending operation. The activity sharply increased in 1973 and 1974, and the unprecedented financing provided in the first six months of 1973 made a contribution which is among the highlights of the bank's history. As bushel volume and the price per bushel increased, the total size of needed loans approached in some instances the system's $195.9 million 1974 commodity loan lending limit to a single borrower.

Farm Supply Operations

Farm supply operations, particularly seed, feed, fertilizer and petroleum products, have held a high place in the lending operations, especially in recent years. Some farm supply cooperatives own major fertilizer plants and petroleum refineries. Some have sizable marketing departments, including grain, and it is not feasible to segregate the loan figures.

Loans to farm supply cooperatives increased sharply in the last two months of 1974, principally as a result of fertilizer and petroleum product operations. At December 31, 1974, the total of loans classed as farm supplies and fertilizer comprised 46.6 percent of the bank's total outstanding participations loans. It is clear today that what was then innovative and courageous financing of major cooperative fertilizer complexes and petroleum refineries resulted in tremendous benefits to farmers of the nation.

The enlarged loan requirements of farm supply cooperatives in relation to the system's lending capacity to a single borrower occasionally resulted in the need to arrange supplemental financing outside the system. This was accentuated since the 35 percent (or $137.1 million) system lending limit usually prevails on loans to farm supply cooperatives. Commodity financing, which permits the 50 percent system limit, is not as extensive as in straight staple commodity marketing cooperatives.

Dairy Financing

The Central Bank has been deeply involved in dairy financing, which always has occupied an important place in system financing. Thus, it played an important role in the growth and development of a number of the nation's large dairy cooperatives. In the six years from 1968 to 1974, the Central Bank's role increased substantially as a result of many mergers of dairy cooperatives.

Fruits and Vegetables

Throughout its history, the Central Bank has been heavily involved both as a direct lender and as a major participant in loans to fruit and vegetable processing cooperatives. Some of the largest and most modern plants in the nation were built with Central Bank financial assistance.

Of particular interest perhaps was the highly receptive mood of the system to large loans for the building of new plants to replace outmoded facilities. This was in keeping with the concept that in food processing only the most modern, sanitary and efficient plants are adequate in the interest of the farmers who produce the crops and the public that consumes the food. Several very interesting financing projects in the 1960s involved groups of growers who were deeply concerned about the maintenance and development of the markets for their products and who joined in major and rapidly expanding cooperative efforts to buy many existing plants to assure and enhance their markets.

In 1974, there was a large increase in loans of this category, reaching 14.1 percent of total participation loans outstanding at December 31, 1974.

Sugar

Sugar factories held an important place in system financing for years. The Central Bank's first cane sugar participation loan resulted in a foreclosure in 1950. Subsequently, however, the assets acquired were sold at a profit.

Major financing of new cane sugar plants started in 1961. When the former great supply of sugar from Cuba no longer was available, growers in the fertile Lake Okeechobee, Florida muckland area were presented with an opportunity to diversify their farming operations. Some innovations in what is described as low equity financing were possible on a sound basis both in Florida and in Louisiana. Growers, who were tied to the factory, were required to make tremendous investments in clearing and planting canelands. Grower groups spent large amounts of their own money for well planned engineering and economic surveys and feasibility studies which proved to be most helpful. In some instances they assumed responsibility by subscribing to stock in their cooperatives sufficient to cover the facility cost.

Another surge of major financing occurred in the early 1970s. In the twelve months ended June 30, 1973, the Central Bank alone made new commitments of $120.3 million to participate in five new accounts. These involved a new cane sugar mill in the Rio Grande Valley of Texas, cane sugar facility financing in Hawaii, the acquisition by a cooperative of a major commercial beet sugar company, and the financing of two new, very large beet sugar factories in the Red River Valley of the north. Some of the financing involved very close working relations between a District Bank and the Central Bank over a long period. This arrangement, which was unprecedented, was necessary in the major efforts to put together sound financing packages utilizing much outside expertise—both engineering and economic. Ironically, sugar prices later rose to very high levels, increasing cash flow to an extent that much of the financing which had been arranged with such great effort was found not to be needed.

Other Farm Products

Cotton financing was one of the single areas greatest in scope in the Central Bank's early history and has continued to be of great importance. In 1974, the banks had an opportunity to consider loans for some innovative operations and processing which conceivably could revolutionize the merchandising of cotton in a part of the Southwest. Oilseed facility and processing financing—cotton, soybean, and flax, for example—has been another area where there was courageous lending.

Wool, many kinds of nuts, broilers and turkeys were a number of the other marketing operations financed. Wool financing in particular took much of the time of the officers over a long period beginning in the early days of the bank.

Transportation

Fleets of barges, long trains, and numerous trucks are essential to the movement of chemical fertilizer from the Gulf and the Atlantic Coast to the interior, of grain to the ports and food products to market. Major amounts of credit have been extended to provide transportation to cooperative borrowers and arrangements have been made to permit leasing as appropriate.

Leverage Lease Financing

Leverage lease financing increased in scope quite rapidly and offered a great potential for a number of major cooperatives. However, the need for specialized expertise is tremendous and the costs involved limit its use to rather sizable ventures. This complicated financing, of course, had a major impact on system staffing requirements.

Rural Electric Association

Rural Electric financing was expected in 1974 to become a more important area of Central Bank participation loans, particularly in generation and transmission projects. In 1974, the Central Bank had only one Rural Electric participation loan. It had, however, engaged a highly regarded consultant and had become deeply involved with several District Banks in considering a number of other projects. This type of financing requires a thorough and open look at the circumstances peculiar to these operations. Their balance sheet ratios and the sources of their basic credit strength are quite different from those of a conventional farm supply or marketing cooperative. The sizable funding often needed had given impetus to the concept of advance capitalization, i.e. an initial investment in capital stock of the District Bank, perhaps as a percentage of the loan. This would prevent undue dilution of the bank's and the system's debt to net worth ratio. How the Central Bank would share had not been determined. This type of financing further illustrates the degree to which the banks have sought to be innovative and receptive to consideration of new credit criteria applied to different situations.

COMMODITY FINANCING

Commodity financing, so essential to farmers' marketing cooperatives, has been a major function of the Banks for Cooperatives.

In the very early years, when the Banks for Cooperatives lacked authorization and adequate funds for this purpose, the Federal Intermediate Credit Banks filled the gap. Later, authority was acquired and the needed loan funds were available. Until 1972, the Central Bank (and thus the system) had no lending limit on commodity loans (or loans on price-supported commodities to the extent of the Commodity Credit Corporation supports) except as was established administratively. In 1974, the limit was $195.9 million for the total of amounts which could be loaned to a single borrower by District Banks and the Central Bank.

There were valid reasons for the greater latitude on commodity loans. Properly handled, hedged and margined and with title documents in the custody of the banks, loans on staple commodities carry a relatively small risk. "Proper handling" is at times quite difficult to achieve. Commodities supposedly in storage may disappear or deteriorate, and on hedged commodities there may be wide swings in the "basis"—the difference between the cash and the future prices. Maintaining the margin may present problems. Consequently, surveillance by a prudent leader is essential.

For many years prior to 1973, the magnitude of the commodity financing by the Banks for Cooperatives was limited considerably because of the big role in this field of the Commodity Credit Corporation. However, in 1973 and 1974, as the activity of that organization diminished, the system had taken over much of this financing with profound effects on loan volume and volatility.

It is largely because of commodity financing that the two-year period of 1973 and 1974 was in many respects the most remarkable period in the Central Bank's history.

CREDIT STANDARDS

A first order of business for the system in 1933 was the development of credit standards. This was a cooperative system effort. The Washington office utilized so-called "coordinators," who spent much of their time in the districts further developing and helping to implement the standards. Over the years, the Farm Credit Administration conducted many conferences on credit. Later some credit conferences were arranged by the banks.

The Central Bank under the successive Commissioners had a most important voice because in the early years it made the larger loans and later had great influence in its role in accepting participations. In its years as a Farm Credit bank the Central Bank followed to a considerable degree the standards which had been built up previously. However, it diligently sought to continue to learn and maintain flexibility to meet varying situations and to adjust its standards with experience.

Teamwork, which is essential, was employed throughout the system. Even highly qualified credit officers, who may be in general agreement as to credit standards, may differ in their views of the proper credit requirements in a given situation. Appraisal of the various aspects, the risks to the banks, and the proper specific loan conditions vary quite widely. The Central Bank found that on occasion standards needed to be tightened as the size of loans became very large. It has been gratifying and reassuring to observe the high percentage of instances where agreement with District Banks was reached in a spirit of cooperation and mutual support.

Notwithstanding considerable pressures from time to time, the Central Bank had no thought of returning to some of the "top down" approaches of the early Federal Farm Board and Central Bank years. It continued its adherence to the concept that a farmer cooperative is a creature of the farmer owners: they must be willing to assume the risk of ownership in spite of the tremendous help the banks can give to the farmers. They should be encouraged and at times perhaps required to have their cooperative build financial strength in which they may take pride and which will permit their cooperative to engage effectively in activities of great benefit to them, either in building markets or reducing production costs. Ownership by the farmers rather than the banks is a difference of great significance. Often, it becomes the point at which the banks have determined what they could appropriately do and what they could not do by way of loan commitments and terms. District Banks on many occasions were most effective in encouraging conditions upon the building of working capital and net worth.

It should be recalled that in general the farmer stockholders in a

Banks for Cooperatives Senior Officer Credit Conference, 1973. Of this group, four became presidents: Howell Hughes, Springfield (first row, sixth from left); Burgee Amdahl, St. Paul (first row, second from right); Jack Hughes, Houston (second row, third from left); and William C. Pendered, Berkeley (back row, third from left). Malcolm Harding (second row, fifth from left) became Governor of the Farm Credit Administration.

cooperative will lose their entire investment before the banks lose a penny. One of the banks' functions is to help farmers recognize an unusual risk so as not to bring capital losses upon themselves. The banks have demonstrated their willingness to take appropriate risks, but cannot expose themselves to undue risk through imprudence. All of their capital funds belong, in effect, to farmers across the nation through their ownership of cooperative locals and regionals and, through them, federations of regionals and, in turn, the District Banks and the Central Bank.

LENDING LIMITS

The participation business of the Central Bank is comprised in the main of portions of loans (overlines) which exceed District Bank lending limits as established by the Farm Credit Administration.[1] The Farm Credit Administration had prescribed no specific lending limit as to the Central Bank in 1947. In 1974, its lending limit on participation loans was \$97.9 million for Class 1, \$137.1 million for Class 2 and \$195.9 million for Class 3, less in each instance amounts carried by the lending District Bank and any other participating banks for Cooperatives.

District Banks' dollar lending limits usually increase each year as their net worth increases. As a result, major amounts of loans move each year to the District Banks. Nevertheless, the Central Bank has grown greatly because farmer cooperatives' credit needs have grown at a more rapid

[1] The dollar lending limits are established by applying a prescribed percentage to the total net worth of the particular bank, usually at the beginning of a fiscal year. These percentages in 1947 were 10, 15 and 25. In 1974 the percentages were 25, 35, and 50. The percentages were applied as follows:

(1) The lowest percentage rate in 1947 applied to loans for the construction or purchase of physical facilities and in 1974 to nearly all loans maturing in over a year and described as "term."

(2) The middle percentage rate in 1947 applied to loans to provide operating capital and in 1974 to seasonal loans in general.

(3) The highest percentage both in 1947 and 1974 applied to seasonal loans secured by eligible commodities and meeting rigid specifications as to loan conditions.

In each instance, the limit was applied cumulatively, the highest percentage limit applied to loans in Class 3 but also to a combination of loans in Classes 3, 2, and 1. The middle percentage limit applied to loans in Class 2 and also to a combination of loans in Classes 2 and 1. The dollar lending limits for the District Bank with the lowest net worth in 1947, depending on the class of loan, ranged from less than \$750,000 to \$1.85 million. In 1974, they ranged from \$3.8 to \$7.5 million. The comparable amounts for the bank with the highest net worth ranged in 1947 from \$1.5 million to \$3.7 million, and in 1974 from \$12.1 million to \$24.4 million.

pace than the District Banks' capitalization and lending limits.

A District Bank for Cooperatives normally is expected to carry on its own loans up to its lending limit. However, exceptions are provided for, subject to approval by the Central Bank. For example, there have been situations where a District Bank wanted Central Bank participation from the start to the extent of 50 percent in a loan to a cooperative which, although relatively small at the time, was expected to grow to a size in excess of the District Bank's lending limit. The District Bank felt that values would accrue to it through the Central Bank's participation.

Provisions also are made for servicing the loans by the District Banks and special arrangements are specified in the event problems develop.

HOW LARGE LOANS HAVE BEEN HANDLED

Handling large loans has been one of the most controversial issues in the bank's history. In 1933, the Central Bank had the exclusive function of handling all large loans on a direct basis. By the late 1950s most loans were handled by the District Banks with Central Bank participation in the larger loans; by 1963, all loans were so handled. Authority still exists for the Central Bank to lend directly to farmer cooperatives if the Farm Credit Administration determines that this would be the best approach. However, the Central Bank in its years as a Farm Credit bank sought to avoid this role.

Between 1956 and 1958, there was strong sentiment that large loans should be handled through the participation of other District Banks with no need for the Central Bank. This issue was resolved in 1958.

Mention should be made that District Banks in general recognized the importance of an objective, independent review of the very large loans. The issue, however, was greatly complicated by the policy of the Farm Credit Administration that it exercise prior approval over all Central Bank participation loans where the loan exceeded the lending limit of the District Bank, which was nearly always the case. Perhaps the duplication of review by two entities from 1956 on was part of the problem.

By the late 1960s, the issue of how large loans should be handled again came to the fore. Cooperatives were growing and their loan needs were increasing. The Farm Credit Administration had made a number of increases in the lending limits of the District Banks, but none for the Central Bank. For the system to handle the size of loans involved, it became increasingly necessary for participations to be sold to a number of

District Banks as well as the Central Bank. There were other actions in the administration of lending limits—the definition of a single credit risk—which had strong influence toward loans being carried by District Banks rather than the Central Bank.

In 1968, as a result of many mergers of cooperatives which transferred loans from one District Bank to another, a policy was adopted as recommended by the Banks for Cooperatives presidents to let a bank which previously had carried the loan retain much of it through participation in the new larger loans made by the lending District Bank. However, as an exception to usual policy, the participating District Banks were to have no authority over credit decisions; these were left to the lending District Bank and the Central Bank.

There was a fundamental issue. The Central Bank staff was mindful of a situation which occurred in the government years where a Central Bank loan which was participated in by several District Banks became a major problem. As is the case in any problem loan, important decisions had to be reached in the loan servicing process. It is reported that one of the District Banks did not concur in any decisions, and ultimately the Central Bank was in effect forced to pick up that District Bank's participation. As authorities in banking are fully aware, for some banks this might be unlawful. In any event, a bank is placed in a very difficult position if it is forced to take such an action. It should be noted, however, that the loan was collected.

Concern was growing over the proliferation of credit decisions which resulted from the increased use of the procedure of spreading large loans among a number of District Banks and the Central Bank. This occurred as the Central Bank Board watched closely the development of a number of serious problem loans and their servicing. The Board and the bank's loan committee were responsible for the loans of the Central Bank. They were of the conviction that this trend had placed the Central Bank in a difficult position and tended to jeopardize the borrower and its farmer members. Widely diffused responsibility may result, in effect, in no fixed responsibility. The issue became quite heated. Proponents of each philosophy were firm in their views. Figures were reported regularly by the Central Bank showing the increasing scope of the problem.

Ultimately, in 1968 the Central Bank Board took a major initiative in regard to an increase in its lending limit. Finally in 1972, the policy was adopted that overall lending limits on a single credit risk, as established on the basis of total adjusted system capital, were to govern in the case of a loan carried by one or more District Banks and the Central Bank.

This was a change of monumental proportions, and it has enabled the system to move forward soundly in the financing of the larger cooperatives. It left open the questions of what to do about the loans already spread out over a number of District Banks. Through 1974, the Central Bank had not sought to upset the existing arrangements but had resisted new proposals from time to time to further spread participations among additional District Banks.

Mention should be made that it was believed that there may be circumstances where the advantages of spreading a loan among a number of District Banks may be greater than the added risks. It should be recognized, however, that the problems and risks to the banks and the borrower may greatly increase, possibly to dangerous proportions, should such a loan become a serious complex problem. Also, there have been situations where the direct or potential impact of problems on a large loan to a cooperative may have had far-reaching effects on its members financed by a number of District Banks and on farmers in a wide area encompassing several districts. In reaching credit decisions some means were devised to harness the combined wisdom of all the banks affected.

By 1974, new developments required revised policy in two areas. First, with inflation and growth, the borrowing requirements of many of the nation's large farmer cooperatives were growing much more rapidly than the capital structure of the system. As a result, the need to seek outside credit assistance—for example, commercial banks, insurance companies or direct placement of securities by the cooperatives—had attained new proportions.

Opinions differed as to how rapidly capital of the District Banks, and thus the system, should grow. Should the system use its full lending limit before seeking outside credit assistance? If not, as the loans approach the system lending limit, at what point should outside assistance be sought? Developments in 1974 were requiring the banks and their borrowers to seek outside credit assistance in an increasing number of instances. Projections made in the Central Bank indicated that this trend would increase quite rapidly and would become a problem for most of the District Banks within a relatively few years.

Second, the system in 1974 was becoming more active in considering loans to Rural Electric Cooperatives, and there was a potential for system involvement in major amounts of generation and transmission financing. It was expected that a large part of the loans would be based upon government guarantees. The Farm Credit Administration ruled that the lending limits of the banks are spread to the extent that loans are government-guaranteed. The question arose, however, as to whose lending limit was spread—the District Bank's, the Central Bank's, or on some pro rata basis. There were also policy questions as to the size and total amount of loans of any category the system may be willing to make.

The manner in which large loans are to be handled will no doubt continue to be a pressing problem for the system in the years ahead.

THE FUNCTION OF THE CENTRAL BANK IN LOAN DECISIONS

In its government years, the Central Bank played a dominant role in credit decisions. As it began to function in 1956 as a Farm Credit bank, ultimately to be owned by the District Banks, there was strong advocacy within the system that the Central Bank adopt a rubber stamp role in agreeing to loan decisions made by District Banks on participation loans. This did not occur. However, with management's basic desire for decentralization and in response to an oral directive from the Farm Credit Administration in the late 1950s that it give the District Banks more responsibility, the Central Bank did move a long way toward following the District Banks.

This represented a deliberate attempt on the part of Central Bank management to help the District Banks develop in their ability in credit by making their own decisions. Notwithstanding, the Central Bank, in keeping with its posture throughout its entire history as an activist for sound credit, agreed to no loan decisions which in its judgment would have placed the Central Bank in jeopardy. The bank was well aware of its special responsibilities in the large loans of the system—working cooperatively with the District Banks—not to agree to unsound credit. The District Banks, of course had the immediate responsibility and in general performed most effectively.

The Central Bank's posture seems to have been sound under the circumstances at the time. It accomplished basic desired results. There were, however, serious misunderstandings of its role. Much of its detailed work on credit was with a very few District Banks. Central Bank posture in relation to the District Banks was also confused by the role of the Farm

Credit Administration in concurrently reviewing participation loans and at times getting out in front of the Central Bank. As a result, a trend developed under which the Central Bank was often bypassed as critical loan decisions were made. This placed the Central Bank staff in a most difficult position.

Thus, by 1970 it had become clear that there was a general system need for greater recognition of the responsibilities of the Central Bank. With Board concurrence, a policy was announced by letter to the President of each District Bank that the Central Bank would not participate in any loan where it was not considered and treated as a full partner with the District Bank. In general, this policy was implemented; however, in 1974 there were some specific areas where further attention seemed needed.

PRIOR APPROVALS BY THE FARM CREDIT ADMINISTRATION

A practice of the Farm Credit Administration during most of the bank's years as a Farm Credit bank was to require that the Administration give prior approval to practically all participation loans of the bank. This practice had an important bearing on the operations and status of the Central Bank.

In the government years, proposed loans which exceeded the lending limit of a District Bank were sent to Washington by that bank for approval. The loan was analyzed and reviewed in the Cooperative Bank Division (later Service) of the Farm Credit Administration. Its analysis and recommendations were forwarded to the Central Bank, which had the option of concurring in buying a participation or taking exception. There followed consultation as required, and a decision by the ranking Farm Credit official who often was also the ranking officer of the bank and thus could speak for both the Farm Credit Administration and the Central Bank. A message was relayed to the District Bank informing that bank of the action taken by the Farm Credit Administration with the notation, "Central Bank concurs."

In January 1956, a major transition occurred to the new role as a Farm Credit bank. The following practice was adopted and was continued in general through 1974: A District Bank seeking Central Bank acceptance of a participation and Farm Credit Administration approval of the loan would make a concurrent submission to the Central Bank and the Farm Credit Administration. The Central Bank would act and relay its action to the District Bank, sending a copy of the message to the Farm Credit Administration. However, the Farm Credit Administration usually was not apprised (1) of the nature of the extended discussions and negotiations which may have occurred between the Central Bank and the District Bank, (2) of additional analysis often made, and (3) of perhaps additional basic new information obtained by the Central Bank. The Central Bank, in view of its relations with the District Banks, saw no basis on which it should volunteer such data. However, it was always receptive to appropriate inquiry. The Farm Credit Administration meanwhile had made such further analysis of the District Bank submission as it deemed appropriate, and, often after extended consultation with the District Bank, took its action. The Central Bank, however, as a general procedure was not aware of the substance of such consultations and perhaps the precise basis for any additional Farm Credit requirements.

There may have been a view that the new procedures in 1956 merely continued in general the procedures in effect prior to that date. However, in a sense they reversed the situation. Prior to 1956, the initial review was by the Cooperative Bank Service and then by the Central Bank. The communications which previously had existed between the Central Bank and the Farm Credit Administration in relation to loan actions generally broke down. This occurred, apparently, not because of a lack of mutual desire for communications but because of factors related to the Central Bank's subtle problem of identity as a farmer cooperative organization akin to the District Banks. The problems which developed between the bank and the Farm Credit Administration may have arisen because of different views as to the intent of the Farm Credit Acts of 1953 and 1955 and their effect on the Administration's previous role as a major loan office.

In the years after January 1956, there were numerous instances when the Farm Credit Administration acted before the Central Bank. This came to the attention of Governor R.B. Tootell, apparently from one of the District Banks, and led to lengthy and detailed discussions with the President of the Central Bank initiated by the Governor. As a result there was a determination that in the future the Farm Credit Administration would not act prior to the Central Bank. In those discussions, the Governor expressed in an informal way a view that perhaps there was no need for any Farm Credit Administration prior approval of the large loans in general. In the Banks for Cooperatives System a procedure had been established for an independent review on behalf of the system through the Central Bank. Ultimately, the Governor indicated that although he felt that the Administration's position in prior approval of nearly all Central Bank participation loans was incorrect, he was not prepared to make a change at the time. However, he gave assurance to the Central Bank that a solution would be worked out by the time the Central Bank retired all of the capital stock owned by the government. This satisfied the Central Bank.

At the time of the discussions, the Farm Credit Administration was the majority stockholder of the Central Bank, a situation which continued until 1965. Until December 1968, it was the largest single stockholder, although technically a non-voting stockholder.

When the Central Bank Board held its regular quarterly meeting in January 1969, the bank had retired all capital stock owned by the government. However, Governor Tootell had announced his forthcoming retirement. The Central Bank Board took the initiative through a lengthy resolution to request the Farm Credit Administration to relax its prior approval requirements, and this resolution was transmitted to the Governor by a long letter from the Chairman of the Central Bank Board, setting forth in full the additional arguments which prompted the Central Bank's request. The Chairman received a most gracious reply from the Governor, indicating that the Board resolution and the material submitted with it revealed very well an important problem of the Central Bank.

Thus, in taking office as the new Governor, E.A. Jaenke had this matter before him for consideration. Later in 1969, there was a significant relaxation by the Farm Credit Administration of its prior approval procedures. It is understood that in 1974, the matter of possible further relaxation was still under consideration. Chart 8 shows the Central Bank's unique position.

The staff of the Farm Credit Administration which reviewed participation loans was in the main dedicated and competent. Their actions at times were very helpful to the bank. However, there were much greater adverse effects as appraised by Central Bank management and Board.

Over the years, in discussions at Central Bank management levels, the view had been expressed that Farm Credit Administration approvals would give the Central Bank protection from criticism when loan prob-

Chart 8
Procedure on FCA Prior Loan Approvals

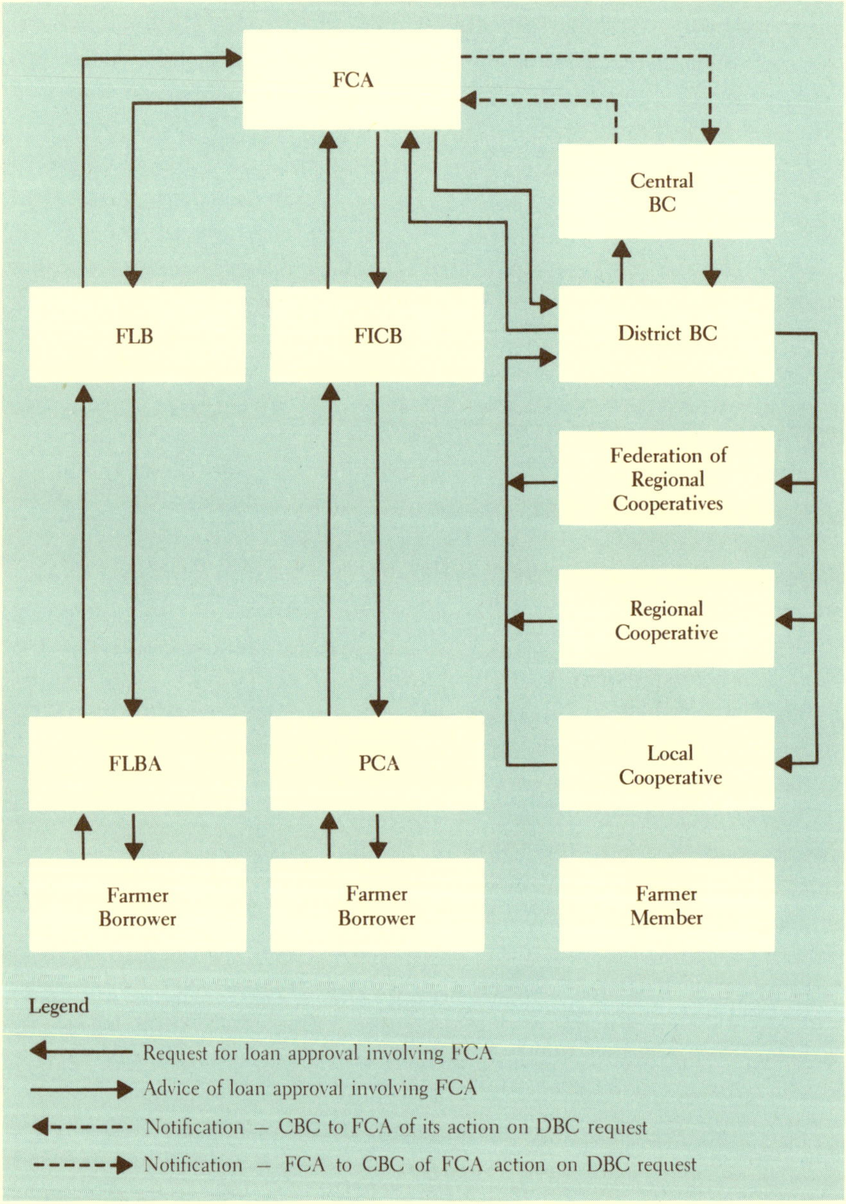

lems occurred. However, years of experience proved quite conclusively that this was not the case. It became clear that the approval requirements on the participation loans, instead of safeguarding the banks as might be assumed, actually in key situations were believed to have placed them in great jeopardy. They were deprived of the right to take action promptly when in their judgment it was essential.

In the event the Farm Credit Administration should take action (as appeared to be under consideration in one critical situation) to take jurisdiction of a serious problem loan, the Administration was handicapped by lack of lending authority and funds. Also, it would be subjecting itself to a possibility of the most severe criticism should a major cooperative be forced into liquidation and/or a serious loss occur to the banks. Even though the handling of the loan had been taken out of the hands of the banks, they still in practical effect would be held accountable by the District Banks and the nation's cooperatives.

Bank management and the Board were thoroughly supportive of the essential need of effective government supervision of the bank through the Farm Credit Administration just as of the other thirty-six Farm Credit banks. However, bank management was also convinced that the participation loan approval procedure was a return to the government years, when the Farm Credit Administration operated the Central Bank. The bank thought the procedure was not consistent with the thrust of the Farm Credit Acts of 1953, 1955 and 1971 and may in fact have impaired in a measure the ability of the Farm Credit Administration to perform its critical role of effective supervision.

The issue presented a very difficult problem to the Cooperative Bank Division of the Farm Credit Administration. There is reason to believe that during most of the period the Administration wanted an overview of all large loans, loans to new organizations and loans to cooperatives with serious problems for the purpose of appraising the ability of District Bank credit staffs in documenting and analyzing such loans, the decision-making process, and the structuring of loan agreements. To the extent weaknesses were found in the lead bank's performance on a case basis, it seemed appropriate from a supervisory level to bring these to the attention of their officers. The review of such loans enabled the Administration to monitor a large proportion of the loan volume in the system with minimal staff. This approach necessarily affected most Central Bank loans.

Over the years the Federal Farm Credit Board was most gracious in affording the Central Bank Board and officers opportunities to meet with the Board. To the extent that details of the prior approval issue were not discussed, some responsibility must rest with the Central Bank. Its management did not have a mutually satisfactory solution to propose. Also, the bank consistently had recognized that the ultimate solution was properly the responsibility of the Farm Credit Administration as the supervisor.

Later, Central Bank management came to the view that in the event a loan required prior approval (of credit factors) by the Farm Credit Administration, the Administration should have the inputs of both the lending District Bank and the Central Bank. Thus, there should be a joint submission (or separate related submissions). This recommendation was made in 1969.

The Central Bank, however, could not really push for a joint submission procedure for two reasons:

1. It might result in delays. This would present no serious problem in most situations; however, it would be critical on occasion.
2. The Central Bank did not have a credit staff of adequate size to carry the added work load if a large number of loans were involved. However, operating on the concept announced in 1970 of being a full partner with the lending District Bank on each Central Bank participation loan a considerable number of participation loan submissions to the Farm Credit Administration for prior approval had many aspects of joint submissions.

From 1956 through 1974 there never was an in-depth discussion of the subject involving all the groups affected, perhaps because there was no appropriate forum for such discussions until the first of the Central Bank's annual stockholders' conferences in 1968 and soon thereafter some steps were underway to solve the problem.

EXPERTISE

One lesson had been learned well as a result of some bad experiences. The system should not finance highly complex facilities without adequate technical expertise. Obviously, the primary responsibility falls on the cooperative which is taking the basic risk of the venture. Nevertheless, the banks should be adequately equipped to ask the right questions and monitor the loans. It was clearly established that expertise was available for these purposes as well as in relation to problem loans, whether in the area of economics, feasibility, engineering, technical industry knowledge, accounting, or legal aspects.

Because of its unique role, the Central Bank naturally had a key responsibility to push hard in this area. It found that, to the extent feasible, expertise should be generated internally. However, it was not possible in all instances, and it was considered a mistake to let prejudices against outside expertise interfere. The bank staff was required to use outside expertise effectively. This is an art unto itself. It includes the ability to properly evaluate what expert help is needed and to utilize special knowledge of experts, but on the bank's terms and under the bank's direction and control without abrogating the bank's responsibilities for its own function. It also involves the ability to terminate the relationships at an appropriate time.

THE CHANGE TO AN INDUSTRY SPECIALIST ORGANIZATION OF THE CREDIT DEPARTMENT

By the early 1970s, it was clear that a reorganization of the Credit Department was essential. A change was made to organize the department primarily by commodity groups or categories of cooperatives. In reaching this decision, care was taken not to revert to a practice used many years earlier which had proved to be unsatisfactory—the placing of credit responsibilities in staff well versed in industry knowledge but not expert in credit. Instead, the decision was reached that the key requirement for men on the credit staff was credit expertise, experience, and judgment. Industry knowledge, while highly valuable, must carry secondary weight. System experience had demonstrated that it was irresponsible to place key credit responsibilities for the large loans on personnel that lacked proper credit expertise and judgment.

PROBLEM LOANS AND BAD DEBTS

A function in which the Central Bank takes great pride is the successful handling of serious problems in cooperation with District Banks, which have the primary responsibility as to participation loans. There is no way the banks can perform effectively and provide the credit service expected of them and yet avoid the adverse results from occasional serious lapses on the part of a borrower's management, from sudden adverse changes in the economic situation, or from sudden and unexpected actions by government regulatory bodies. Also, at times there was inadequate credit administration.

Thus, troubles have come. Considering the risks taken in financing major projects in the interest of farmers, the hazards beyond the control of a borrower and the number of critical problems which developed over a period of some forty-two years, it is significant that the actual charge-offs of bad debts were held to some $200,000 net over the entire period. There were, however, at December 31, 1974 some serious problem loans, and a reserve of $14 million for bad debts had been provided. The reserve amounted to 9/10 of 1 percent of the outstanding participation loans.

There were a number of reasons for the bank's good record in avoiding losses. The times were generally favorable; there was only limited exposure to fraud. But there were other major factors: (1) The general posture of adequate loan analysis and sound structuring; (2) the pattern of aggressive servicing combined with consideration, great patience and understanding and the acceptance at times of major added loan risks in a sincere desire to reach an ultimate solution in the best interest of all concerned; and (3) the financial strength of the bank and the system which permitted the acceptance of the high dollar risks. Also, in every time of unusual loan increases, attention was given to the basic question of the soundness of the bank's credits. The Central Bank in cooperation with the District Banks utilized at times special teams of experts for this purpose. As a result, some corrective actions were taken on a timely basis. It would be difficult to find another major bank where such a high proportion of the time of its top officers over such a long period was devoted to the satisfactory working out of serious problem loans.

A *Summary of Problem Loans*

Perhaps some additional detail regarding problem loans would be of interest. In the Central Bank's government years, there was a continuing stream of serious problem direct loans. This was not unexpected, considering the circumstances under which the bank was operating; it was organized in a depression period. There was much of the "top down" Federal Farm Board philosophy at the start, and it took time to establish sound credit policies.

There also were a number of serious problem participation loans. Two of these resulted in losses charged off—the only charge-offs the Central Bank had ever taken. One, in 1952, was on a loan to a farm machinery cooperative. Another, in 1951, was on a loan to a fruit-processing cooperative. In a third situation, a loan to a cane sugar cooperative, properties acquired in 1950 in foreclosure later were sold at a profit.

Since 1956 a number of serious problem loans have involved potential losses of millions of dollars. For example, in the late 1950s and the 1960s, there were in succession two most serious problems—one a Central Bank direct loan and another a participation loan which took much of the time of the bank officers but which ultimately worked out very well.

As the bank approached and entered the 1970s, the situation changed and for the first time in its years as a Farm Credit bank the bank experienced a considerable number of serious problems concurrently. This taxed the bank's limited staff. By December 31, 1974, great progress had been made in the marked improvement or the working out of most of these problems.

Methods Used

Handling a serious problem participation loan becomes a joint responsibility of the lending District Bank and the Central Bank, and often requires the presence of a bank representative at the Association's offices. A custodian to maintain a clear lien on and control of the Association's current assets and to provide valuable liaison between the borrower and the banks worked to mutual advantage in some circumstances. A loan representative on location sometimes was the answer. In one recent serious situation, a three-man loan servicing team was devised, with one officer on location. Frequently outside expertise must be employed.

Usually it is necessary at some point to make available substantial additional loan funds, and this decision becomes very difficult. The bank prides itself on the tremendous additional risks which have been taken. On occasion these have proven to be in the best interest of the banks, the borrower, its members, and the whole area which it served. Through 1974, there had been no instances where the added risks had proven to be unwise. They had been a key factor in the bank's record of having sustained no charge-offs in its entire nineteen years of experience as a Farm Credit bank. The contribution made to avoiding scandals and catastrophes which would have been harmful to cooperatives in general was of tremendous proportions.

The question arose at times as to the procedure which would be followed if the lending District Bank and the Central Bank (or any participating District Banks in some instances) could not come to agreement as to a course of action. The participation agreement between the banks provided that in the event of such a problem on a loan which was in default, as defined by the agreement, the question would be referred to the Farm Credit Administration and its decision would be final. During the entire period of 1956 through 1974 this procedure was not used except in the case of one serious problem loan, where the Central Bank had the major risk and some aspects of the procedure were employed. The problem was resolved very satisfactorily.

Over the years, the bank gained an expert ability to work constructively with the lending District Bank. Each satisfactory solution added to the confidence and prestige of the bank, and was helpful in permitting the bank to exercise the aggressiveness, the patience, and perhaps the added dollar risk often necessary.

SUMMARY

The Banks for Cooperatives claimed that they offered the best financing package available anywhere to farmer cooperatives. A sterling feature in regard to the larger loans was the banks' record of devoting the resources needed—personnel, outside expertise, and dollars—to see cooperatives they had financed through tough problems. Their posture was to lay down tough requirements under which the cooperative could help itself with bank patience and forbearance, but yet stern discipline. The pattern served borrowing cooperatives, their farmer members, and the banks well.

One of the great appeals of credit work with the Central Bank has been the opportunity to participate in the rapidly changing, highly complex and difficult decisions in the whole spectrum of credit operations. The Central Bank serves as a bank of participation and thus does not obtain the direct exposure to the same degree as one of the District Banks, and also does not obtain the same degree of recognition from the borrowers. Nevertheless, the sense of achievement to the Central Bank credit staff has been an important work incentive.

The bank is proud of the cooperative spirit in which it sought to respond appropriately to all requests from District Banks for eligible financing, always attempting to keep in mind the true interest of the farmers served.

7

Great Adventures in Funding

GENERAL

The bank has taken great pride in its smooth funding operation over so many years, and particularly since January 1973, as the Banks for Cooperatives System assumed a major portion of the financing of farm commodities previously handled by the Commodity Credit Corporation.

In a letter of May 2, 1973, Governor E.A. Jaenke of the Farm Credit Administration wrote to the President of the Central Bank:

> All of us in the Farm Credit Administration recognize that recent weeks have been a time of unprecedented demand on the Banks for Cooperatives and particularly the Central Bank. Were this known generally, farmers and their cooperatives would be deeply grateful for the outstanding way you and your staff have performed in this time of extreme need.
>
> But in addition to this tremendous performance, the Central Bank for Cooperatives has assisted all of the Banks in fostering the most efficient use of System funds possible on a day-to-day basis. The Federal Farm Credit Board is aware of this important service and at the meeting here a few days ago, adopted a resolution of appreciation for the help of your Bank in promoting a smooth flow of funds among the Farm Credit Banks for maximum benefit to the Nation's farmers and ranchers.

The magnitude of the Central Bank's participation loan operation and the lack of a regular, predictable seasonal pattern are shown by Chart 9. At times, as in the 1973 grain financing, the Central Bank performed a major role in providing funds to District Banks for unexpected needs.

The following discussion is intended primarily for those with a special interest in Farm Credit finance.

Years of Development

The capability in financing which was demonstrated in 1973 and 1974 did not happen accidentally. It was acquired from many years of seeking and arranging financing options, establishing adequate commercial bank borrowing relationships, obtaining authorization—with the full cooperation of the Farm Credit Administration—to utilize some new sources in obtaining loanable funds, and through the Farm Credit System "money desk" operation which marshalled system surplus funds. The increasing flexibility in financing afforded by the Farm Credit Act of 1971 was invaluable. The capability was sharpened through many trials over a long period.

In 1933, the bank relied for lending funds on monies which could be salvaged and drawn from the revolving fund. Starting in 1943, seasonal swings were met to an increasing degree by commercial bank borrowings. The first issue of Central Bank bonds (debentures) was sold through the fiscal agency in 1950. Through 1954, the entire Banks for Cooperatives System was financed to a major extent by the Central Bank. In 1955, there was the first issue of consolidated bonds by the thirteen banks.

The consolidated bonds became the most important source of funds to finance the Banks for Cooperatives System. They were issued on behalf of the thirteen Banks for Cooperatives by their fiscal agency in New York City, which served the same function for the Federal Land Banks and the Federal Intermediate Credit Banks. Each of the thirteen Banks for Cooperatives was primarily responsible for its own share, but all thirteen were jointly and severally responsible for all of their system's bonds.

The advent of consolidated bonds and each bank's ability to raise funds through bonds on its own behalf resulted in a natural period of confusion. The District Banks for Cooperatives had been relying heavily on the Central Bank as a financier and continued to do so in varying degrees.

Chart 9
Outstanding Central Bank Loans to Cooperatives

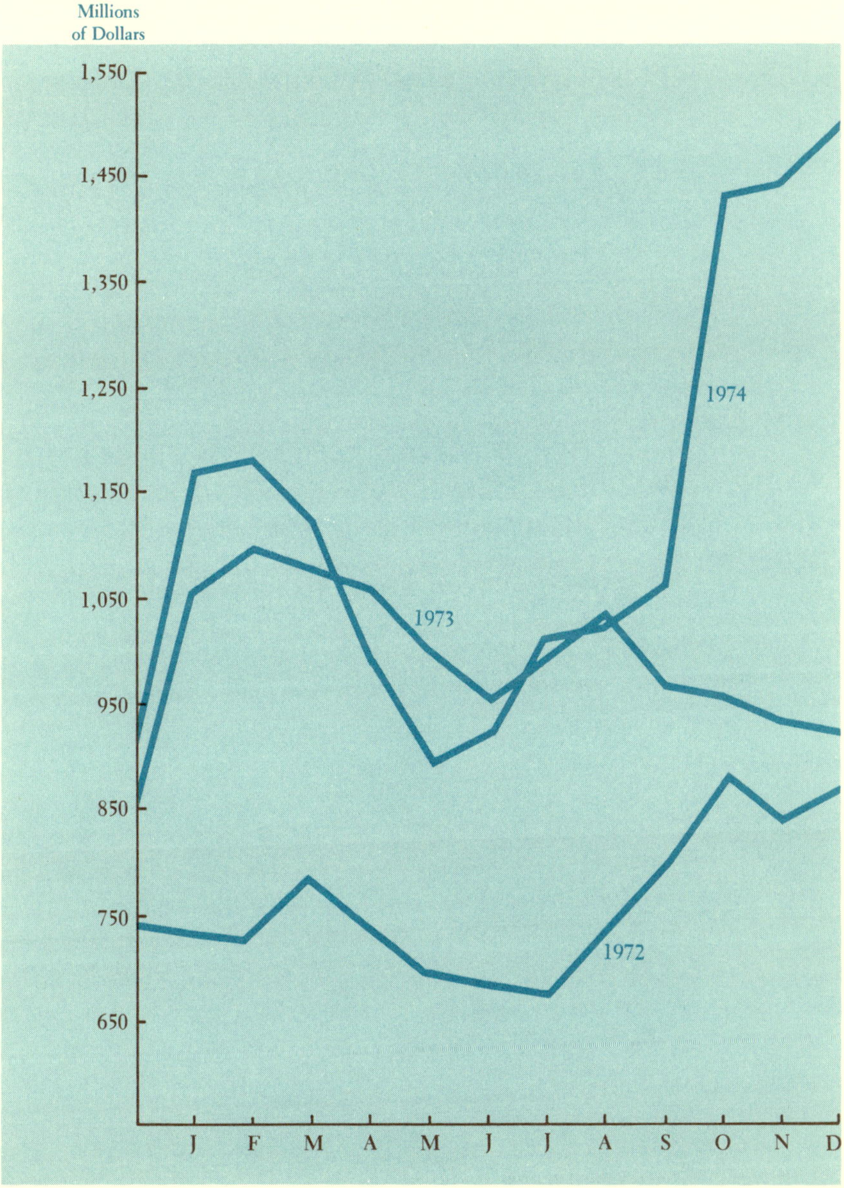

A Basic Change

In time, a basic change was agreed upon. Each District Bank would finance its own loan operations through its participation in consolidated bonds issued plus borrowings from commercial banks and other Farm Credit banks. The Central Bank (although no longer the principal financier) would provide funds to District Banks for Cooperatives for use in financing loans which they carried themselves in case they had no other readily available source of funds. That was necessary on a number of occasions. Sometimes the Central Bank borrowed large amounts of funds for that purpose.

In 1960, the Banks for Cooperatives System embarked on a pattern of six annual issues of six-month bonds; in 1966, this was increased to eight issues, in 1968 to ten issues, and in 1974 to an issue each month—a tremendously gratifying development. The pattern of six-month maturities provided a most convenient means of adjusting outstanding bonds to fit seasonal swings in need for funds. The short-term issues were supplemented to a degree by longer term issues, and the system was committed to further extending its debt. For many years, the Central Bank had been a consistent advocate of a good blend of longer term issues. One deterrent was the need of the system to first have the volume required for a sizable six-month issue each month to facilitate marketing—an imperative not attained until the 1970s. The Central Bank preferred five- to seven-year or longer maturities when feasible rather than a uniform pattern of three-year maturities when bonds of terms longer than six months were issued.

Occurrences which placed the Central Bank on its mettle and helped to develop its financing capability included the dock strike which started in January 1965. In planning the amount of bonds to be sold February 1, almost everyone estimated that the strike would be short. Instead, it was long. Commodities built up on wharves and in railroad trains on sidings to the extent that embargoes were placed in effect at seaports. Demand for funds became greater than ever before. Apparently no other bank in the nation was affected so greatly. The commercial banks with which lines of credit were maintained were sympathetic and helpful, and increased the credit lines to $141 million, a tremendous sum at the time for the Central Bank of that day.

The "credit crunch" of 1966-1967 presented a new problem. It was the first time since the bank began issuing bonds that its access to the market was regulated by action of the President of the United States, even though for a very brief period.

Increasing Magnitude of Variations in Seasonal Financing

The first indication of the trend to much greater fluctuation occurred in the corn blight year of 1970, when outstanding participation loans increased by $322 million or 55%, a much larger seasonal increase than ever before experienced. There was a challenge in financing because the unprecedented summer loan upsurge occurred before the system had attained monthly entry to the bond market.

A reverse twist occurred the following year. Financing was based on the prospects of another corn blight year. This did not develop, resulting in much lower loan volume and thus larger amounts of surplus funds than had been planned.

Then came January 1973. Nothing in the bank's previous experience was comparable. For a period there was a daily outpouring of Central Bank funds of about $30 million. System outstanding loans to cooperatives increased $511 million in that one month. The Central Bank provided much of the money. This called for a thorough appraisal of how the financing would be handled. New sources of borrowing (including loans from some government agencies) were utilized. The heavy demand for funds continued for several months owing to purchases of grain from farmers at the high prices available, transportation tie-ups related to the Russian wheat sale, and hedging margins.

In July and August 1973, the system again was faced with an unprecedented seasonal need for funds to finance wheat sold by farmers to their cooperatives, causing an overall increase of loan volume instead of an expected downtrend. The amount also was greater than in previous years because of the larger number of bushels and the much higher price. The experience of wheat harvest was expected to be repeated at the time of corn and soybean harvest, and funds estimated to be needed were obtained from the sale of bonds. However, farmers tended to hold their corn and soybeans and major amounts of surplus funds resulted.

January 1974 was another month of system loan increase somewhat larger than 1973, but there followed heavy seasonal loan liquidation.

Then in the months of October to December 1974, participation loan volume increased $441 million, with farm supply cooperatives accounting for the largest portion.

The magnitude of fluctuation in interim need for funds and their general unpredictability are the key factors which make the Central Bank's financing unique. There is no way of being certain whether loan volume will increase or decrease. Often it is not possible for the borrowing cooperatives to predict accurately when farmers will sell their grain and other commodities, what the price will be, what effects will result from weather, when the farmers will be paid, when the commodities will be sold and shipped and the proceeds collected. As just one illustration, large loan repayments result when one or more ships are loaded for export, but the exact time of this loading is not known far in advance.

Required Hedging Margins

The need for funds to finance hedging margins presented another imponderable. For example, in 1973 the demand for funds for hedging margins was extremely high when soybeans moved from $5 to $12 a bushel and corn, wheat, and cotton increased greatly in price. A marketing cooperative, as the owner of the commodity, would protect its position by selling "short." It is estimated that the Central Bank at times during the first six months of 1973 had over $100 million, or more than 10 percent of its total volume in loans to finance hedging margins. In the event these funds had not been provided on a timely basis, cooperatives could have suffered financial disaster.

Assume for example that a marketing cooperative had acquired five million bushels of soybeans at $5 a bushel. To offset its resulting long position, suppose it sold futures at $5.30. If the market moved up $3, the cooperative may have had to pay a total of some $15 million to maintain its hedged position. A failure to have done so could eliminate the sought-after hedged position and bring loss to the cooperative.

Assume that five cooperatives were concurrently in a comparable position. A total need for funds would have been $75 million. A failure to raise such funds could have a "domino effect" of most serious proportions.

The Shift from "Short" to "Long" Money Posture

This change was a profound development. By the late 1960s it was becoming apparent to bank officers that it was not sound to finance through commercial bank borrowings the loan variations between dates of issues of bonds (referred to in the system as "going short"). It was not feasible to maintain commercial bank lines large enough for this purpose and provide also an added cushion for contingencies. The cost would have been prohibitive. It was becoming clear that a greater degree of liquidity appropriate to the growing lending operation was essential. A basic change was triggered by developments which resulted in the Central Bank's having in 1967 some $80 million of temporary surplus funds at the height of the first credit crunch. After months of study, it was decided that in the future a basic posture of greater liquidity should be maintained by selling enough bonds at each issue date to provide the funds estimated to be needed until the next bond issue date (referred to as "going long").

Concurrently, it was necessary to make arrangement to invest on an advantageous basis the resulting temporary surplus funds to the extent these were not used for "demand" loans to other Farm Credit banks. Investments through repurchase agreements played an important part. Repurchase agreements—referred to as "repos"—represent the purchase of securities under an agreement that they will be repurchased by the seller on a fixed date and at a fixed price so as to provide the purchaser a rate of interest yield agreed to at the time the transaction was negotiated. Under the new flexibility of the Farm Credit Act of 1971, overnight unsecured investments with commercial banks at federal funds rates assumed key importance.

TEMPORARY SURPLUS FUNDS IN THE FARM CREDIT SYSTEM

By the 1950s, it had become increasingly clear within the Farm Credit System that it would be mutually advantageous if temporary surplus funds of any of the thirty-seven banks were used in the system by cross-lending and borrowing among the banks. Legislation ultimately expanded previous limited authorizations to full authority. As a general practice, these funds were loaned at rates somewhere between the lending rates of commercial banks and the investment rates for short-term funds, i.e. on United States Treasury bills or comparable investments.

The Central Bank was a major borrower of surplus funds, primarily from the Federal Intermediate Credit Banks, which had heavy seasonal loan liquidation in the fall when the Central Bank seasonal loans reached their peak. The Intermediate Credit Banks financed production; the Banks for Cooperatives financed marketing. The Banks for Cooperatives, although heavy on the borrowing side, were short on the lending side.

When the Central Bank made its first loans to District Farm Credit Banks other than Banks for Cooperatives, it ran into some policy questions. The District Banks for Cooperatives, as the part owners and prospective full owners of the Central Bank, naturally desired preferential interest rates and other preferential treatment. This was fully understandable; however, it presented problems to the Central Bank because it was advantageous to maintain reciprocal arrangements with other Farm Credit banks.

In the late 1950s, the Central Bank was experiencing wide fluctuations in its borrowing pattern. Research developed the fact that the Central Bank, in effect, was carrying much of the daily swings of the entire Farm Credit System. For example, when a Bank for Cooperatives would find money available from other banks in the system, it often would borrow those funds to repay the Central Bank. Then when a call was made for repayment of funds, the Central Bank was asked to provide the monies. This situation was explained in detail to a group of Banks for Cooperatives Presidents, leading to better understanding and to voluntary decisions on the part of the District Banks for Cooperatives to curtail the procedure.

During the 1960s there was intense competition for surplus funds among Farm Credit banks. Often there were extensive individual communications as to the rate. The Central Bank in general was expected to be the last taker of funds; that is, District Banks were given first opportunity and the Central Bank sought not to compete with them. This, however, was difficult and costly, at least to the Central Bank and probably to the system. The Farm Credit Administration became a mediator—surplus funds were reported to it and it determined which banks should have a call on the funds.

How borrowed surplus funds helped to cover the Central Bank's "short" money posture is illustrated by Charts 10 and 11, which show the

Chart 10
Funding Pattern, 1962-1964

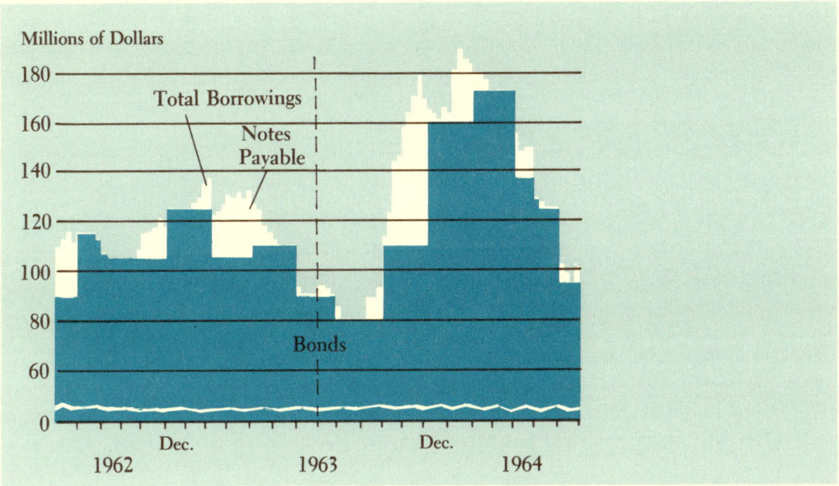

Chart 11
Composition of Notes Payable, 1962-1965

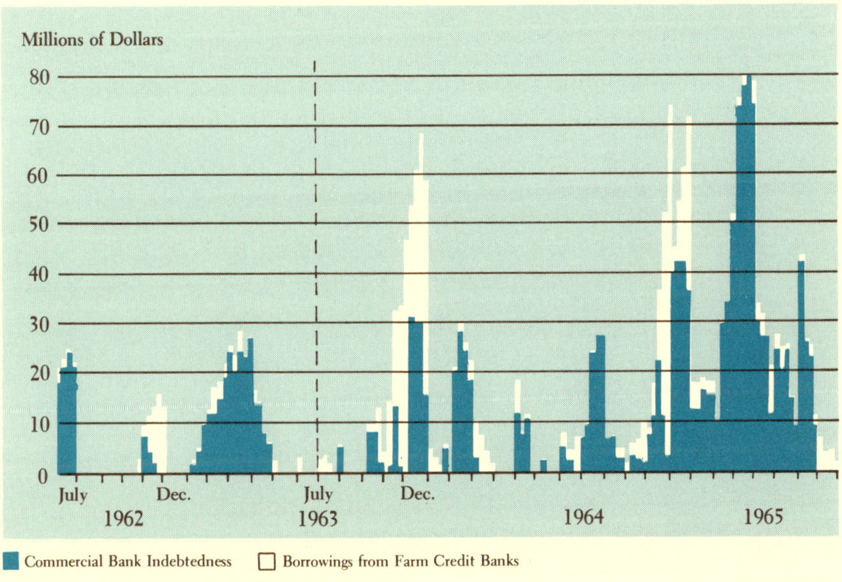

basic funding pattern from 1961 through 1964 and the composition of the notes payable item in the first chart. As system surplus funds could be borrowed, notes payable to commercial banks were repaid.

As a general practice, when surplus funds of a Farm Credit bank could not be used within the system, they were used to retire system bonds before maturity by purchase on the market.

In 1967, during the first credit crunch, some Farm Credit banks were out of funds and the Farm Credit Administration appropriately restricted the retirement of bonds before maturity and sought to achieve equity among Farm Credit banks by taking firm command of the surplus funds of the entire system.

At about the same time, an unusual happening occurred. After the Central Bank had determined the amount of bonds to be issued, there was mutual agreement that two of the larger borrowers would obtain needed funds from the Commodity Credit Corporation rather than from the Banks for Cooperatives as previously planned. As a result, some $80 million of surplus funds developed at the Central Bank. These were offered to other Farm Credit banks but meanwhile were invested in "repos." Although the Central Bank had previously used the "repo" method of investing temporary surplus funds, at this time it embarked on this course in a major way and thus was a leader in the system in that area.

In 1969, the Farm Credit Administration determined to discontinue its role in regard to the administration of surplus funds and have this function handled by the fiscal agency. In October a letter was sent from that agency to each of the banks in the Farm Credit System setting forth the procedures to be followed. The new procedures particularly a new rate-setting procedure by the fiscal agency, on borrowings of interbank funds, resulted in significant changes to the Central Bank. In essence, each District Bank, after checking with the two other banks in its district, was to report surplus funds to the fiscal agency. That agency would arrange loans to other Farm Credit banks or make investments, through "repos," on behalf of the bank which owned the surplus funds.

The Central Bank followed the sense of this procedure to the extent which it was feasible without impairing its ability to operate economically and maintain adequate liquidity.

The fiscal agency did the excellent job which would be expected in making investments on behalf of the banks. However, banks frequently placed "repos" with relatively long maturities and it often occurred that other banks were in need of funds, and called upon the Central Bank for loans at times when there were major amounts of surplus system funds tied up in "repo" investments. The fiscal agency was handicapped by inflexibility owing to the fact that its "repo" transactions were settled at the New York Federal Reserve Bank under strict eastern time zone limitations. A bank such as the Central Bank had to give a firm answer whether it wanted a "repo" investment before the start of its active financial transactions for the day. Often it had no way of knowing.

The new procedure appeared to significantly reduce the extent to which system surplus funds were used in the system — they tended to end up in term "repos." Also, the Central Bank was greatly handicapped in its traditional role on behalf of the District Banks for Cooperatives and in being able to borrow system surplus funds as in the past.

Report of "Blue Ribbon Committee"

In 1970, the report of the Advisory Committee on Finance appointed by the Farm Credit Administration contained seven recommendations, one of which was that "Non-productive funds should be minimized by the more efficient management of cash flows. A central pool is recommended for this purpose."

The report clearly indicated that the operation would be handled by the fiscal agency or a successor corporate organization. There was a supporting comment of no present consequence but reported as fact. Upon some inquiry, it seemed clear to the management of the Central Bank that those who had represented the banks in providing information to the Committee were not well informed on the operations of the Central Bank in the area of system surplus funds and of its view that a majority of the system's investments of surplus funds and the termination of such investments[1] were handled on a timely basis — certainly those of the Banks for Cooperatives system and the other Farm Credit banks that worked closely with the Central Bank.

[1] The term "investments" is used loosely to include demand loans to the Central Bank.

Management of the Central Bank was deeply concerned at the prospect of placing in an agency not under its own control and direct accountability the critical responsibility for maintaining its day-to-day liquidity and that of the Banks for Cooperatives System, where it had a traditional responsibility. That system was subject to unpredictable day-to-day volatility in demands for funds far in excess of that of either of the other two systems within Farm Credit. Liquidity had been based to a considerable degree on the availability of system surplus funds. However, there would be time for system study of that issue and, if adopted, the establishment of needed "machinery," policies and plans for accountability for day-to-day liquidity.

For the short term, management of the Central Bank was convinced that the immediate activation of the recommendation, perhaps through requiring full compliance to the fiscal agency procedures as mentioned, would be disruptive to normal operations and possibly inhibit the ability to meet loan demands.

Thus, in the interest of sound short-term as well as long-term decisions, the Central Bank arranged a meeting with high level officials of the Farm Credit Administration to clear up obvious misunderstandings which existed. Those officials were not aware of the extent of the Central Bank's involvement in borrowings from and loans to Federal Land Banks and Federal Intermediate Credit Banks as well as Bank for Cooperatives. Neither did they know of profound changes which had occurred in the ten-year period which had elapsed since a comparable comprehensive study had been made by an internal committee of the Farm Credit Administration.

The outcome of the meeting was that the management of the Central Bank felt it had a carte blanche to proceed for the time as in the past with direct borrowings from and lendings to District Banks for Cooperatives and other Farm Credit banks at their option. There resulted by far the smoothest surplus funds operation in Farm Credit history—far more effective than could have been accomplished through a "pool of surplus funds," at least as that term was understood in Farm Credit circles—and the greatly increased liquidity which was crucial to the Farm Credit System in 1973 and 1974.

EVOLUTION OF THE FARM CREDIT SYSTEM "MONEY DESK"

With the latitude just described, an increasing number of District Farm Credit Banks loaned their surplus funds to the Central Bank and borrowed from it when they were in need of temporary funds. The Central Bank accomodated all those banks when feasible. These borrowings and loans generally were repayable on call. As a result, the Central Bank attained greater flexibility in funding its volatile participation loan operations. The Central Bank was operating as a "banker's bank." Each District Farm Credit Bank retained the full responsibility for its own funding operations and did business with the Central Bank when it served the District Bank's interest. There developed a rewarding degree of cooperation. Individual District Banks were most gracious in providing funds to the Central Bank when it was in need; the Central Bank reciprocated, and the Farm Credit System "money desk"[2] gradually evolved. It developed not as the result of a plan but rather in response to a mutual need. A serious void had existed and the Central Bank reacted in its own interest and that of the Farm Credit System.

A concept of the dollars involved in 1974 may be gained from Table 12.

Table 12
Farm Credit System "Money Desk" Operations, 1974

Credit extended to:	
Banks for Cooperatives	$877 million
Federal Land Banks	535 million
Federal Intermediate Credit Banks	575 million
Total Farm Credit Banks	$1,987 million
Funds borrowed from:	
Banks for Cooperatives	$984 million
Federal Land Banks	609 million
Federal Intermediate Credit Banks	653 million
Total Farm Credit Banks	$2,246 million

[2]The term "money desk," which originated in the Farm Credit System, is used with great reluctance and strictly in the interest of brevity. The term is not really descriptive; however, no simple alternative term had come into use.

Table 13 shows average outstanding "money desk" loans and borrowings from 1970 to 1974. This further demonstrates the degree of reciprocity. In comparison with Table 12, it provides a concept of the degree of turnover of funds.

Table 13
Average Outstanding Loans to and Borrowings from District Farm Credit Banks
1970-1974

Fiscal Year [a]	Banks for Cooperatives	Federal Intermediate Credit Banks	Federal Land Banks	Total
		millions		
1970				
Average loans to	$17.2	$ 5.7	$ 5.8	$ 28.7
Average borrowings from	$ 3.5	$ 5.1	$ 1.5	$ 10.1
1971				
Average loans to	$30.2	$ 4.9	$ 4.2	$ 39.3
Average borrowings from	$ 5.2	$16.9	$10.9	$ 33.0
1972				
Average loans to	$36.7	$10.9	$12.9	$ 60.6
Average borrowings from	$ 7.8	$13.1	$ 5.1	$ 26.0
1973				
Average loans to	$53.4	$ 7.0	$ 9.4	$ 69.8
Average borrowings from	$ 9.8	$37.8	$16.0	$ 63.6
1974				
Average loans to	$22.7	$31.7	$20.9	$ 75.3
Average borrowings from	$23.6	$14.9	$16.2	$ 54.7
July-December, 1974				
Average loans to	$23.0	$10.6	$31.6	$ 65.2
Average borrowings from	$51.0	$54.1	$98.4	$203.5

[a]Twelve months ended June 30.

The long years of study and experimentation had shown that a satisfactory Farm Credit System "money desk" operation, if conducted by the Central Bank as in 1974, required that it seek to maintain a planned liquid money position appropriate to the overall Central Bank and system situation. Also the Central Bank must be prepared either to borrow or to lend at the same rate. It must borrow system surplus funds as they become available and in anticipation of needs and plan to pay an interest rate at or sufficiently above the market to draw the monies. It must borrow outside the system on occasion in addition to issuing bonds. To reduce its surplus funds when this seemed advisable, it would lower the interest rate to or somewhat below the market. This would discourage District Banks from loaning their surplus funds to the Central Bank or encourage them to borrow from the Central Bank. Adjustments of money positions sometimes required seeking the cooperation of Farm Credit banks through requests for specific actions.

Obviously, District Farm Credit Banks benefitted from these policies. A key question is how the Central Bank gained. It too, was helped because a soundly administered "money desk" operation kept Farm Credit System surplus funds available as needed to the Central Bank and the entire Farm Credit System. Experience clearly proved that this permitted the Central Bank to handle its volatile and often unpredictable participation loan business with relatively small commercial bank backup lines ($203 million in 1974). Also, these lines were seldom used and thus served as a cushion for contingencies and were less expensive to maintain.

Charts 10 and 11 illustrate Central Bank financing from 1962 through 1965 on a "short" money posture. However, no charts are included illustrating financing on a "long" money posture in conjunction with the "money desk" even though experience has indicated quite clearly that it is difficult to understand the operation without a series of complementary charts. Good visual data have been available for several years at the Central Bank for general use within the Farm Credit System and are presented periodically at appropriate internal meetings. These have been omitted here because they show the varying funds positions of the other two systems within Farm Credit as well as those of the Central Bank and the Banks for Cooperatives System.

In summary, the "money desk" has resulted in better utilization within the Farm Credit System of the temporary surplus funds and increased liquidity systemwide.

Successful operation was dependent on good communications. Thus each week Farm Credit banks voluntarily provided to the Central Bank information about their money position. This information as system summaries was made available to all the banks, the fiscal agency and

Farm Credit Administration. In addition, there was good communication through monthly letters and telephone discussions.

Incident to the "money desk" operation, the Central Bank assumed a responsibility to provide interim financing not only to District Banks for Cooperatives, as in the past, but to any District Farm Credit Bank in case of need. In reciprocity, District Farm Credit Banks have been most helpful to the Central Bank when it was short of funds.

It was the Central Bank's view that perhaps any of the very large Farm Credit banks could have performed the "money desk" function. However, the Central Bank was especially well equipped because of its self-interest. It needed to finance its very large and unpredictable daily participation loan activity. The "money desk" operation made possible the continuation of its traditional direct loan and borrowing services for its owners, the District Bank for Cooperatives. The Central Bank's back-up lines of credit from commercial banks and its $156 million capitalization (1974) provided financial strength to support its commitments to stand back of any Farm Credit bank for needed interim funds if it was not feasible to obtain them from other sources.

THE FISCAL AGENCY

A key factor in achieving success for the entire funding operation was the maintenance of fine relations and close cooperation with the fiscal agency which arranges for the marketing of the system's bonds through a nationwide group of securities dealers and dealer banks. This is the principal source of funds for loans—sometimes referred to as the "life blood" of the system.

The agency, located in New York City, is governed by a fiscal agency committee comprised of three bank presidents and four District Bank directors. Of the three presidents, one is a Federal Land Bank President elected from their number, likewise a Federal Intermediate Credit Bank President and a Bank for Cooperatives President. The four District Directors are designated at the National Farm Credit Directors' Conference. The fiscal agent who heads the staff is selected by the committee.

In each of the three systems (Federal Land Bank, Federal Intermediate Credit Bank and Banks for Cooperatives) a bond committee has jurisdiction over pricing and maturity of bond issues.

Special mention should be made of new circumstances in 1975 with the system entry into the commercial paper market through short-term discount notes offered by the Fiscal Agency on a weekly basis on behalf of the thirty-seven Farm Credit Banks. These, no doubt, will have important effects on the Central Bank's pattern of financing between bond dates.

The Staff of the Fiscal Agency in 1974. Seated in front, left to right: Mrs. Gisele Andersen, Supervisor-Budget & Accounting; Mr. Aubrey K. Johnson, Fiscal Agent; Mrs. Helen Orzel, Receptionist-Clerical; Mrs. Delores Santa Lucia, Clerk-Stenographer. Standing: Mrs. Emma Conboy, Administrative Assistant-Marketing; Mrs. Connie Figliuolo, Clerical Assistant; Mr. Gerald F. Kierce, Deputy Fiscal Agent; Mr. William E. Pettigrew, Financial Economist; Mrs. Doris L. Ross, Office Manager-Executive Assistant.

The remaining Fiscal Agents who served for extended periods since 1950 when the first Central Bank bonds were issued.

McDonald G. Newcomb, 1949-1955.

John T. Knox, 1955-1967.

Glenn G. Browne, 1968-1972.

Note: Robert W. Gilmore served during parts of 1967 and 1968.

CAPITALIZATION OF THE CENTRAL BANK

In 1933, the basic decision was made that it was not economical for each District Bank to maintain a capitalization which would permit it to handle on its own the very large loans in the district. Instead, there should be a separate single large pool of capital at the Central Bank through which these loans could be handled on a less costly basis. Through 1955, the Farm Credit Administration and other Federal officials determined the allocation of available capital from the revolving fund and resolved the highly emotional issues which developed.

With the Central Bank's new status on January 1, 1956, the issue again became sensitive because of inequities in the distribution of Central Bank net savings and differences in view as to whether the Central Bank was needed. A satisfactory interim solution was reached in 1958 through the $24 million of low rate allocated loans by the Central Bank to the District Banks. These were repaid by 1966.

Base Capital Plan

In 1968, a new Central Bank capitalization plan was adopted—the "Base Capital Plan."[3] This required an amendment to the participation agreement (the contractual relationship between the District Banks and the Central Bank under which it handled participation loans). The amendment provided that the District Banks could be assessed by the Central Bank annually or more often for capital needed by the Central Bank as determined by its Board of Directors with the approval by the Farm Credit Administration. The allocation to the District Banks was based on participation loans sold to the Central Bank over a period of years—originally ten, then nine, then eight (in 1974). The objective was to reduce it to five. Under this new arrangement, the capitalization of the Central Bank at December 31, 1968, was established at $91.4 million. There were annual increases as follows: 1969—$8.6 million; 1970—$6 million; 1971—$6 million; 1972—$5 million; 1973—$11.5 million; 1974—$12.5 million. As a result, the basic capitalization for the fiscal year 1974-1975 was $141 million. However, with current accumulations through operations, the bank's net worth in December 1974 was $156 million.

[3]Previously the bank's capital plan provided for the revolving of equities into cash, just as was the case in the District Banks. However, there had been no such revolving.

There were several aspects to the operation of the plan. Nearly all District Banks required their borrowers to make periodic investments in capital stock of the banks in amounts related to interest on the loans. In the case of participation loans, a pro rata portion was used by the District Banks in turn for investment in the capital stock of the Central Bank. In general and in total for the twelve District Banks (except in 1968) these investments were more than adequate to meet the increased capital needs of the Central Bank called for in the annual capitalization under the base capital plan. Thus, a portion was refunded to the District Banks. Also, again in general and in total for all District Banks, the year's patronage refund was in effect made in cash.

Level of Central Bank Capitalization

From organization in 1933 until the 1970s, the Central Bank was heavily capitalized in relation to loans. This is illustrated by a comparison of loans (to cooperatives) and net worth (total capital accounts) at December 31 and the ratio of loans to net worth, given in Table 14.

Table 14
Level of Central Bank Capitalization

	1935	1945	1955	1965	1974
			millions		
Loans to cooperatives	$19.6	$73.5	$76.8	$313.2	$1,500.2
Net worth (total capital accounts)	$73.9	$91.9 [a]	$80.9 [a]	$ 91.4	$ 156.3
Ratio of loans to net worth	0.3/1	0.8/1	0.9/1	3.4/1	9.6/1

[a] The bank, as a financer of District Banks for Cooperatives, in earlier years also had loans to them of $10.2 million in 1945 and $66.4 million in 1955.

There were a number of reasons for the heavy capitalization:

1. In the early years, capital was the only source of loanable funds.
2. Later, large capitalization was necessary to have lending limits on a single credit risk of adequate size to permit the Central Bank to provide

the credit service to cooperatives expected of it. This was consistent with the concept of one large pool of capital. Lending limits were established as a percentage of net worth.

3. The Central Bank had to maintain its ability to honor its undisbursed loan commitments. These had tended to approximate in amount its outstanding loans. Thus, the 8 to 1 statutory system limitation on outstanding bonds to net worth which was in effect from 1954 to 1971 ultimately posed the threat of a limitation on lending not believed by the banks to be justified. The 20 to 1 limitation provided by the Farm Credit Act of 1971 solved this problem.

4. Previous experience in the Farm Credit System and the projections by Dr. L. L. Boger indicated clearly that capital needs would develop more rapidly than capital was being built. Therefore, it was essential to continued good service in the future to build capital as this was feasible.

In 1974, the retiring President of the bank was of the view than an appropriate ratio of loans to net worth had been attained considering the risks at that time in the lending operation and the need for some margin for commitments and contingencies.

CAPITAL COMMITTEE OF THE CENTRAL BANK BOARD

The creation in 1968 by the Central Bank Board of a Capital Committee of the Board proved to be a momentous event. The committee performed two basic functions. It made annual recommendations to the Board as to the capital needs of the bank for each fiscal year starting July 1, 1969, under the annual capitalization plan, and it delved into all aspects of capitalization and funding. The committee met annually in New York City. It visited with major commercial banks, security dealers, the fiscal agency and on occasion the Federal Reserve Bank. Its purpose was to study and obtain counsel on capital adequacy, explore and evaluate possible new funding options and obtain a broad background in finance. The committee met at times in Chicago for the same general purposes and arranged to meet in 1975 in San Francisco.

The work of the Capital Committee was instrumental in identifying and obtaining authorization, through the Farm Credit Act of 1971 and Farm Credit Administration authorizations thereunder, of major funding

Capital Committee of the Central Bank Board, 1974. Left to right: Melvin E. Ensley, Dr. Howard F. Robinson, Darrell D. Moseson and Joseph A. Kyser.

and investment options which have been of great value to the bank and the system. One of the options diligently sought but not obtained was authority to issue unsecured capital notes. It was thought that this opportunity should be available whether or not it was determined that it would be used. As to the bank staff and directors, reference is made to the committee's May 1970 report, a copy of which is in the bank's files.

The reports of this one committee illustrate the constructive work over the years of so many "in house" Farm Credit committees which has so clearly demonstrated the capacity of the system to effectively use experts and find solutions on its own to many of its pressing problems.

Dr. L. L. Boger, consultant to the committee, served in a unique role. While Dean of Agriculture and Natural Resources at Michigan State University, he served as a member of the Central Bank's Board of Directors from 1967 to 1971. He was a member of the Capital Committee from the time it was organized in 1968 until 1971, when he became chairman. After leaving the chairmanship he began his service as a consultant.

His efforts in projecting the capital needs of the Central Bank and the Banks for Cooperatives System was invaluable. This work took the form of a book, *Furrows on the Street–Now and 1985*. The book broadened the horizons of thinking within the system and pointed the way to greater

Dr. Lawrence L. Boger,
Consultant to the Capital Committee.

emphasis on both innovative, sound projections and capital development. The presentations Dr. Boger made at the bank's annual stockholder's conferences profoundly influenced the decisions made to permit the progressive substantial increases in the bank's capitalization which occurred.

Dr. Boger was active at Farm Credit meetings across the nation both as a featured speaker and as an active and influential participant. He served as a member of the Commission on Agricultural Credit which functioned in 1969 and 1970.

Composition of the Capital Committee (through 1974)

John T. Lesley, 1968-1971, Chairman 1968-1970
Dr. L. L. Boger, 1968-1971, Chairman early 1971, then Consultant.
H. Allan Segraves, 1968-1969
Melvin A. Ensley, 1970-1974, Chairman 1973
Glen R. Harris, 1971-1973, Chairman late 1971 and 1972
Darrell D. Moseson, 1971-1974, Chairman 1974
Dr. Howard F. Robinson, 1972-1974
Joseph A. Kyser, 1974

GRATITUDE TO THE NATION'S FINANCIAL COMMUNITY

For many years the bank has maintained excellent and substantial relations with major commercial banks and through the fiscal agency with important security dealers. It has been traditional to seek their counsel in regard not only to capital adequacy and funding techniques but also in many other phases of operations. Their gracious and constructive advice has been most helpful to the bank in establishing policies and improving operations. Such assistance has been supplemental to the major financing which they have provided or facilitated over the years.

8

Other Developments and Problems

LOCATION OF THE CENTRAL BANK

Initially, the Central Bank was located in Washington D.C. It was designed as a government bank and operated within the Farm Credit Administration. At January 1, 1956, there was serious consideration of a relocation to Chicago. However, the decision was reached that the Central Bank would move its offices from Farm Credit Administration headquarters in the Department of Agriculture, South Building to rented quarters in downtown Washington, D.C., the Pennsylvania Building.

By 1968 there was consensus that the bank should be moved to a more central location. The law, however, referred to the Central Bank for Cooperatives, Washington, D.C. It seemed imprudent to request special legislation; however, ultimately, the Farm Credit Act of 1971 authorized relocation as determined by the bank's Board of Directors with the approval of the Farm Credit Administration. In 1972, after a thorough study of alternatives, the bank relocated to Denver, Colorado. It had been decided that it should not be located in the headquarter city of any of the Farm Credit Districts. For other reasons, certain other cities were determined as unsuitable. The ultimate choices became Milwaukee, Memphis, Dallas, and Denver. Experience has demonstrated clearly the wisdom of the move from the standpoint of status as a Farm Credit bank, staffing, relations to participation borrowers and convenience in day-today financial operations. In regard to the latter, the Central Bank was surprised to find that notwithstanding the fact that its primary banking relations were in New York City, a location in the mountain time zone made life much easier for the treasurer's staff. The intensive day's financial arrangements were concluded by normal lunch time in the mountain area—2:00 p.m. eastern time.

STAFFING, DEVELOPMENT AND TRAINING

For years, the Central Bank operated with a very small staff in relation to dollar volume. This was possible because the basic loan analysis and servicing was done by the District Banks. However, the Central Bank remained fully responsible for its participation loans, and it conducted a sizable financing operation. As a result, the qualifications for its staff were exacting.

Even though the number of personnel was inadequate, the work that needed to be done was accomplished. However, it placed a heavy burden on individual officers and employees and prevented the carrying out of desirable staff training and development programs. Also, it precluded a number of foreign and other special assignments which would have been valuable to the bank.

Four events radically changed the situation.

1. In 1972, the Central Bank Board realized that the Central Bank must offer higher salaries than any of the District Banks for Cooperatives. Most of the credit officers of the Central Bank were recruited from the District Banks, where they had gained the basic knowledge and experience necessary for the Central Bank role, and a higher salary level was necessary to facilitate such recruitment. In 1972, a differential was authorized.

2. The relocation from Washington D.C. to Denver, Colorado in 1972 also facilitated recruitment of top staff.

3. Fringe benefits comparable to those of the District Banks were developed. The Central Bank's staff was too small to permit it to do much on its own except in regard to joining a local group to obtain group hospitalization and major medical coverage. For other programs it was invited to join in the plans of one of the Farm Credit Districts and was dependent on their lead. In time, however, a good overall program was in effect.

4. A somewhat larger, highly qualified staff was authorized to properly carry out the special functions and responsibilities of the Central Bank. Clearly, the work of the Farm Credit System Management Development Study Committee was very beneficial. A member of the Central Bank Board, Director Ensley, was chairman of the Committee. In response to a request from the committee, the Central Bank reported a total of twelve as of January 1, 1973, in the combined categories of senior officers, junior officers, and technical staff members. It reported, however, that the bank was six short at that date, and that the numbers should increase further by January 1, 1978. A justification was provided for the estimates. The report was made available to the Central Bank Board and was favorably received.

To a considerable degree, staff development was accomplished on the job, and efforts were made to see that each officer and employee had ample opportunities for improvement. For many years, it was the policy of the bank to encourage and pay the expenses of professional development programs such as those provided by the American Management Association, universities such as Harvard Business School, and special training in new concepts such as leverage leasing; also funds management, training as executive secretary and the like.

However, the extreme work load of the relatively small staff prevented for many years the optimum use by staff of these educational opportunities. With the increase in staff in 1972 through 1974, this problem was alleviated greatly.

A key event which helped set staff direction was the "retreat" at Rehoboth Beach, Delaware, about 1970, for all senior officers. Out of this came a clear affirmation as to the importance of the work being done and constructive plans for improved performance.

THE STRUGGLE TO INCREASE NET SAVINGS AND THE RETURN ON CAPITAL

There were many obstacles, including the high capitalization of the Central Bank until the 1970s in relation to loans, which reduced "leverage"; the low interest rates on loans; and the $24 million of very low interest rate "allocated loans" to District Banks for Cooperatives from 1958 through 1966.

A boost was given in 1971 by the elimination (on recommendation of the District Banks) of compensation for their servicing of participation loans at the rate of 1/4 of 1 percent of the principal.

It was not until the fiscal year ended June 30, 1974, that the Central Bank attained a rate of return on capital deemed by management to be acceptable.

THE SUBTLE PROBLEM OF IDENTITY AS A FARMER COOPERATIVE ORGANIZATION

A number of factors have made it difficult for the Central Bank to shed an illusive and seemingly pervasive image as a government bank as distinguished from a cooperative organization.

Its succession in the 1930s to some of the Federal Farm Board heritage for years led some influential individuals to be greatly disappointed and at times quite forceful when the bank refused their requests for what the bank viewed as "hand-out" actions not consistent with its farm credit role. The passage of time finally cured this problem.

The twenty-three years (1933-1955) as a government bank and an integral part of the Farm Credit Administration followed by more than sixteen years in which the bank continued to be headquartered in Washington, D.C. During most of this latter period the Farm Credit Administration continued to insist on requiring its prior approval of nearly all participation loans of the Central Bank. As just one illustration of confusion there was an instance in the late 1960s when the Central Bank had agreed with a District Bank to accept a participation loan and the Farm Credit Administration is believed to have made additional requirements. The District Bank complained to the Farm Credit Administration that "Washington" should get together and approach the District Bank with one voice. There apparently was no consideration at the District Bank or the Farm Credit Administration of the Central Bank's view that the District Bank and the Central Bank, having come to agreement, should then jointly approach the Farm Credit Administration with a single voice. It is difficult to estimate the degree to which this problem may persist. In any event, "identity" was a distinct problem during most of the experience of the Central Bank through 1974.

TAXATION

During the government years the Central Bank was exempt from income taxes. From 1954 through 1968, it was subject to a federal franchise tax and paid $8.2 million in such taxes. Since 1969, after the final retirement of all capital stock owned by the government, it has been subject to both federal and state income taxes. The transition to this new status presented serious technical problems affecting all of the thirteen banks.

To help meet the issues, Governor A.E. Jaencke appointed a tax committee of Bank for Cooperatives' presidents, including B. H. Schulte, Berkeley, J. R. Williams, Wichita, and Homer G. Smith, Central Bank, Chairman.

The committee concluded that in addition to the use of competent accounting firms for tax service, there was a need for highly competent tax counsel for the entire Banks for Cooperatives System. Upon authorization by the presidents, the committee engaged system tax counsel. The combination of the two types of tax service proved to be appropriate and invaluable.

There followed a period of great mutual effort to clear all the complex problems. The most difficult problem technically was in the area of the patronage refunds from the Central Bank to the District Banks and the Central Bank's annual recapitalization (Base Capital Plan). An internal revenue ruling was obtained to achieve a satisfactory solution of that problem.

ANNUAL STOCKHOLDERS' CONFERENCES

Seven of these conferences were held between 1968 and 1974. They proved to be the most important annual event for the Central Bank. Over a period of a day and a half, Board and staff reported to the twelve District Banks, and the pressing issues of the day were discussed with representative directors and the president of each of the twelve District Banks. These were the only such forums in all of Farm Credit. Also, they provided the Central Bank its first opportunity since 1957 to present to its owners as a group, in an appropriate setting, its operating results, problems and plans for the future. There also were opportunities for input from members of the Federal Farm Credit Board and officials of the Farm Credit Administration. In recent years, there has been representation from the presidents and other officers of the Federal Land Banks and Federal Intermediate Credit Banks.

A key item on the agenda was the projections of Central Bank and system loan volume and Central Bank capitalization for the ensuing year based on Dr. L. L. Boger's work as consultant to the Board's Capital Committee. At the 1970 and 1971 conferences, major attention was given to needed legislation to afford greater options in funding, and to correlate Bank for Cooperatives statutes with income tax laws. Discussions of the growing size of loans, lending limits, and how large loans should be handled have taken an important place. There have been panel discussions participated in by Directors and Presidents dealing with pressing issues. Occupying an important place on the program each year were detailed explanations of the Central Bank's financing pattern, basic changes which have occurred, and the "money desk" operation.

A general view, 1973; pictures from the conferences.

Another general view.

The Fiscal Agent speaks.

Governor Jaenke of the Farm Credit Administration addresses the Conference.

District Directors took an important part.

Dr. L. L. Boger ponders "Furrows and The Future."

John Harling, President, Omaha, makes a point.

FARMBANK SERVICES

At the close of the period covered by this history, a new organization called "Farmbank Services" was being established by the banks of the entire Farm Credit System. Its function would be to provide services to banks and associations or groups of them, at their option, on a better and more economical basis than could be done by individual banks. This organization, the outgrowth of years of study and endeavor by the banks, was to headquarter in Denver, Colorado.

Farmbank Services, it was believed, was destined to provide invaluable services to the Farm Credit System.

9

The Central Bank — A Considered Combination of Centralization and Decentralization

THE ROLE OF THE CENTRAL BANK

It seems clear that the founders thought of the Central Bank, to be run by the Farm Credit Administration, as a key institution in the Banks for Cooperatives System. It was established by Title III of the Farm Credit Act of 1933, whereas the District (or regional) Banks were established under Title IV.

The bank was created to make the larger loans to cooperatives, but from 1937 to 1963, its role changed to that of a participant in the larger loans made by the District Banks.

In 1933, it was given the sole authority to issue bonds (debentures) and in the early years was a major financier of the District Banks. By 1954 neither was the case. Ultimately its Farm Credit System "money desk" assumed importance.

The bank in 1974 did not occupy the same kind of position it held from 1933 to 1955, but it rendered a more important service in permitting the District Banks to arrange the financing in great measure of the very large farmer cooperatives. Although it exercised increasingly a voice in the basic credit decisions, clearly it enhanced even to a greater degree the stature of the District Banks.

As cooperatives increased greatly in size, sophistication and complexity, as loan volatility grew, and as critical loan problems developed more frequently, it appears that system views evolved to the point of perhaps universal recognition that the Central Bank was essential. Cooperating with the District Bank, it contributed greatly to sound credit judgments in difficult areas, the efficient handling of interim needs for loan funds, and to working out satisfactorily the very serious large problem loans.

THE IMAGE OF THE CENTRAL BANK

In 1933, the Central Bank had very high visibility. In the ensuing years, as the District Banks began handling more of the loans to cooperatives, there were discussions at Board meetings as to how strong support could be maintained for the Central Bank. For example, in September 1939 there was a proposal at a Board meeting that the Central Bank should have about fifty direct loans rather widely scattered to aid in this purpose. Ultimately, however, the decision was reached that the system would move in a different direction and that the Central Bank would become a bank of participation in District Bank loans.

It seems quite clear that some of the relationship problems with District Banks which developed in 1956 and the ensuing years were due to the high visibility the Central Bank was attaining, as well as the prestige its new president had acquired in his work across the nation in regard to the Farm Credit Act of 1955 in his role as Deputy Governor of the Farm Credit Administration and Director of the Cooperative Bank Service.

Two basic decisions were reached informally. First, the Central Bank would cooperate fully with the District Banks in resolving satisfactorily the basic questions which concerned them, regardless of the effect on the Central Bank. Second, the Central Bank would desist from activities which might be construed as seeking to enhance its visibility vis-a-vis the District Banks. Thus, the *Central Bank News* was discontinued. Nearly twelve years elapsed from the first stockholders' luncheon meeting in January 1957, to the first of the seven annual stockholders' conferences starting in 1968 and continuing through 1974. Central Bank officers would be most careful in regard to speaking engagements which they were requested to make. None would be accepted except on the invitation of the individual District Bank or at least with what was deemed to be its wholehearted encouragement.

A posture developed to concentrate on excellence in performance with low visibility. This posture served the Central Bank and the system well through 1974 and resulted in the ability of the Central Bank to accomplish more for the Banks for Cooperatives System, the entire Farm Credit System and the farmers of the nation than would have otherwise been feasible or possible in the context of the system politics.

In 1975, a new day had dawned, calling perhaps for new solutions.

A CONSIDERED COMBINATION OF CENTRALIZATION AND DECENTRALIZATION

A great deal of the Central Bank's success is attributed to the gradual achievement of what is considered a generally sound balance between individual District Banks' prerogatives, authorities, and responsibilities under their own boards and officers and those which should be exercised by the Central Bank.

In the lending operations involving participation loans, meticulous attention was given by the Central Bank toward achieving this result. Only a District Bank could initiate a loan. As the lending and servicing bank, it understood the area situation and the needs and desires of the farmer members. The Central Bank, on the other hand, has a broad overview; its lending policies should be more closely attuned to the overall system. In any event, it has the full responsibility for the funds it makes available to the borrower through participation; thus, it has a controlling voice at least by way of veto or the imposition of loan conditions. By policy, it insisted on being a full partner with the District Bank in the financing. However, it diligently sought not to overstep its powers and prerogatives.

These relationships, properly applied, helped to develop new concepts in lending and yet maintain a soundness and stability. They helped District Banks to grow and develop. They kept the Central Bank on its mettle, responding to the requests of the District Banks and seeking to concur in their proposals yet without agreeing to loan decisions which in its judgment were unsound or which involved excessive risk to the Central Bank.

That plan made it necessary for the Central Bank to walk a most difficult tightrope. It placed great stress on the bank's staff and at times created problems in staff relations with the bank's board.

In the "money desk" operation in behalf of the thirty-six District Farm Credit Banks, each of the banks maintained its autonomy in finance under its board and officers, and yet it had the benefits of flexibility in placing its surplus funds, the utilization, as needed and available, of system surplus funds, and a call on the Central Bank for interim financing. The Central Bank viewed its role as a conduit to a degree with a principal objective of taking courses which would result in system surplus funds being available for use within the system. It sought to see that each bank was knowledgeable of system funds, positions, and alternative opportunities and the financial advantages which accrued to each bank which utilized the Central Bank's services.

Both in credit and funding, the Central Bank contributed to decentralization and sought to pursue centralization only to a necessary degree.

10

What Has Been Accomplished For the Nation and Its Farmers 1933-1974

The Banks for Cooperatives System has been a boon to farmers seeking to establish and maintain markets, reduce their costs, and increase their income through cooperative effort—a self-help basis. Through loans of some $23.6 billion at most favorable interest rates, the Central Bank played a major role in such assistance to the larger farmer cooperatives across the nation. There is no question that the progress of these cooperatives and their contribution to the income of the nation's farmers have been much greater than would have been possible without the system. The growth of the larger cooperatives has in large measure helped to strengthen many of the smaller cooperatives, and farmers in general have been served.

THE CONTRIBUTION OF FARMERS' COOPERATIVES

In addition to their effect on members' incomes, farmer cooperatives have had an impressive impact on the international supply of food and fiber. It is difficult to conjecture conditions which would have existed had the cooperatives not been successfully established. Their role in processing and marketing farm products such as fruits and vegetables, dairy, sugar, oil seeds and grain has resulted in wide distribution, and the products are found in the supermarkets and grocery stores of the land.

Quality seed, feed, fertilizer and petroleum products provided by farm supply cooperatives have added spectacularly to the production of farm products for use both domestically and in export.

The Central Bank takes pride in the major facilities which have been financed through the help of the system—some of the largest and most modern in the nation. The great fertilizer complexes have been dedicated to providing plant nutrients for American farmers. If these nutrients had not been available in 1973 and 1974, American agricultural production would have been substantially reduced, resulting in a major adverse effect not only on the world-wide production of food and fiber but also on the balance of payments, which has been aided greatly by American agricultural exports. In 1973 and 1974, the system was perhaps the most active financier of sugar factories in the world. The impact of these facilities on the world supply of sugar has been and will be increasingly significant.

VALUES ACCRUING FROM A DEPENDABLE SOURCE OF CREDIT AND SOUND LENDING

The benefits to farmers and their cooperatives from the dependable source of loanable funds available from the system is incalculable. The Central Bank's role on occasion has been crucial. Farmers found immeasurable the value of the funds available for their grain cooperatives in the first six months of 1973 to finance the flood of grain sold by farmers and to finance required hedging margins.

The beneficial effect to farmers of sound loan policies and professional loan servicing is inestimable. In agreeing to credit, the banks gave careful attention to the value to farmers measured to a degree by their willingness to assume the risks of ownership of their cooperatives. It is no credit to a bank to agree to financing which leads to loss of the capital invested by farmers or their farm products or their source of farm supplies. The dangers of a "top down" approach were learned well.

Farmers have benefited greatly from the successful handling by the banks of so many critical loan problems. Aggressive yet sympathetic loan servicing and courageous but carefully calculated inputs at times of major amounts of new funds produced constructive results.

It is more than fortuitous that from 1956 through 1974 the Central Bank did not have to face a single situation where it forced a borrowing cooperative into liquidation or where foreclosure was resorted to in liquidation of its loan. Concerted effort at times was exerted to avoid financial catastrophes which would have been harmful to a particular cooperative and its members and to farmer cooperatives in general.

CONTRIBUTION TO AGRICULTURAL LEADERSHIP

One area of service, often overlooked, is the degree to which stronger farmer leadership has developed through the participation of farmers as directors in the major business enterprises financed by the banks and on the bank boards.

"FURROWS ON THE STREET"

Dr. L. L. Boger's book, written in his role as advisor to the bank's Capital Committee, relates to the high degree to which American cooperative farm leadership, through their Farm Credit associations, became knowledgeable in finance and the workings of the money and capital markets of the nation. Many farm leaders, traditionally suspicious of Wall Street, have gained a high degree of respect for its great value. Likewise, the "Street's" close working with Farm Credit has contributed to its understanding and appreciation of American agriculture.

CONTRIBUTIONS TO SOUND COOPERATIVE ORGANIZATION

A farmer cooperative can be an excellent form of corporate organization if it serves effectively, with farmer ownership and control, a vital economic role to its owners as an integral off-farm part of the farm operations. The system has contributed by exercising major influence in promoting sound cooperative management and operations.

DIGNITY AND SATISFACTION

In addition to the economic benefits which accrued to farmers, there has been a considerable contribution to their dignity and satisfaction resulting from the success of cooperatives which farmers owned and controlled.

11

Contributions to the Farm Credit Heritage

A priceless asset of the Farm Credit System derives from the contributions which it has made to the nation's agriculture over a period of some sixty years through the operations of the Federal Land Banks and Associations starting in 1917, the Federal Intermediate Credit Banks in 1923 and the Production Credit Associations and Corporations and the Banks for Cooperatives in 1933. The good that has resulted is immeasurable.

The system's heavy government orientation during long periods has given way, through system insistence, legislative policy, and practice, to complete farmer ownership and a high degree of farmer control. This did not just happen. Tremendous grass roots efforts and dedicated leadership were required at various periods. Over the years farmers of the nation were offered the opportunities and challenges of ownership and major control. They proved worthy of the high privilege.

The Central Bank for Cooperatives evolved from a government bank to an impressive farmer-owned bank, taking its place with the other thirty-six Farm Credit banks. The bank, cooperating with the District Banks, rendered a major credit service consistently dedicated to the objective of helping farmers build and maintain sound cooperatives which they owned and controlled to supplement their on-farm operations. The many instances of constructive help by the banks when over some forty-two years large farmer cooperatives have encountered serious difficulties is recognized by some national financial leaders as perhaps unprecedented in major lending operations.

The Farm Credit System has a reputation for innovative credit service combined with soundness. The Banks for Cooperatives System in considerable measure pioneered in developing policies and techniques for the sound financing of farmer cooperatives.

The banks and associations of the Farm Credit System have built impressive capital structures consistent with their growth and have created funding techniques which permit borrowing on most favorable terms their needed loan funds through their own fiscal agency. Thus, they have maintained a dependable source of credit so essential to agriculture.

The Farm Credit record truly constitutes a heritage to be treasured.

12

Opportunities and Challenges Ahead

The future of the farmers' cooperatives of the nation and of the Banks for Cooperatives is closely related. Perhaps never before were farmer cooperatives receiving so much praise and yet so much criticism as in 1974. The praise resulted from the tremendous job done in providing fertilizer, petroleum products, and other farm supplies to farmers at a time of great need. The monumental efforts in building the great manufacturing complexes dedicated to providing for the needs of farmer members were paying handsome dividends. Canned and frozen fruits and vegetables, dairy products and farm commodity marketing had helped to avoid even greater shortages than otherwise would have resulted. Continuing criticism arose from ill-advised acts of a relatively few individuals in milk cooperatives.

The challenge for the cooperatives is to build on their record to avoid the mistakes of the past and take appropriate steps to tell their impressive story and systematically build the best possible public relations.

The future of the Banks for Cooperatives will be determined by the effectiveness of their service to the farmer cooperatives of the nation—not only those operating in 1974, but those yet to be organized. This will depend in large measure on how the banks meet the following challenges.

Effective Functioning of the Boards

Of critical importance is the determination and ability of the boards to continue their development in competence and stature consistent with the growth of the banks. Great responsibility goes back to the membership and the power of election.

Adequate Staffing, Development and Training

This is a matter of highest priority. Only top quality staff can meet the rapidly increasing size, complexity and to a degree, the growing risk of loans. The highest possible level of continuous development and training is essential for staffs to keep up with "new technology" in credit, cooperative operations and funding and yet retain sound principles.

Specialization in Constructive Credit and Appropriate Loan Policies

Loans constitute the banks' business, and critical loan decisions require the best efforts of top flight credit officers under well thought-out policies and with sound legal counsel. The quality of a credit man should not be measured by how easily and emphatically he says "no." Instead, it should depend on his skill in soundly evaluating and structuring difficult credit packages and helping to figure out ways to strengthen them. His function should be positive. It is essential that past problem loans be studied and that credit policies be designed and employed to avoid repetition. Skills must be continuously developed to handle effectively new serious problems as they may develop.

One clear lesson has been learned. With the increasing size and complexity of loans and the degree of concentration of risk, there can be no tolerance of lower than top levels of expertise. Truly professional stature is essential for both the bank staff and outside consultants engaged.

The Highest of Business Ethics

Some potential conflicts of interest are inherent. It is imperative that this continue to be recognized and discussed openly to facilitate positive action to preclude any abuses and to minimize the possibility of any appearance of improper actions.

Strict Confidentiality

The banks necessarily are privy to a great deal of highly confidential information. They must continue to maintain a spotless record in treating unpublished financial or other credit information confidentially.

Needed Funding and Capitalization, Financial Strength and Liquidity

Notwithstanding the tremendous strides over the years, funding continues as a subject for top study and consideration. Policy as to speed at which net worth will be built should have high priority. The system in 1974 was not growing in capital structure as rapidly as its borrowers' needs for loans. The maintenance of strong and growing capitalization is essential if the system is determined to maintain its credit service during the growth years ahead. There is no room for complacency since increases in capital at a slower rate than inflation would result, in practical effect, in a reduction of capital. The bank has demonstrated its dedication to appropriate liquidity. However, continued attention is essential. There can be no tolerance of any failure to meet commitments.

Closely related is the matter of "pricing policy" on loans. In 1973 and 1974 the interest rates were far below commercial banks' prime rates. No assertion is made that this was wrong. It is merely suggested that there should be continuous thought of whether the banks should follow the traditional cooperative policy of charging competitive rates and adjusting to cost by the patronage refund. If so, determination must be made of what is a competitive rate. Then, of course, there is the question of what portion of the net savings should be retained and what portion paid out in cash.

Appropriate Board/Management Relations

Bank management must respect the responsibilities and prerogatives of the Board. Board members, or the Board itself, must continue to resist the natural temptation, at times, to seek to work out critical loan problems by direct action, or otherwise usurp the responsibilities of management. Instead, management must be required to work out the problems (under Board policies) and be held accountable for results.

Cohesive and Appropriate Relations between District Banks and the Central Bank

Considering the structure of the system, the continuation and improvement of its record of service calls for a fine balance between the prerogatives and responsibilities of the District Banks and those of the Central Bank.

A sound policy must be maintained in regard to the handling of large loans. This must be determined on the basis of what is right for both the District Banks and the Central Bank and best for the farmer cooperatives and their members.

Mutual understanding, good working relations and the spirit of teamwork must be constantly improved. These are responsibilities not only of credit officers and loan committees but also of Boards of Directors. The Central Bank Board must play an important role in this area.

The plan will work only if there are twelve strong District Banks as well as a strong Central Bank. The view was taken by the Central Bank that, should there have been District Bank weakness, consideration might have to be given to some restrictions in the approach to lending.

Good Member and Public Relations

The banks, just as their cooperative borrowers, must give adequate attention in this matter. Basic of course, is sound and constructive operations in the interest of the nation and its farmers and ranchers. Appropriate efforts must be made to achieve positive public relations.

A Constructive Attitude Toward Change

This book chronicles the significant changes over some forty-two years of system operations and the many and at times painful adjustments which have been made. Basic system objectives and goals as reevaluated from time to time must continue to govern and thus facilitate the many further changes to be anticipated in the years ahead.

Continued Effectiveness of the Farm Credit Administration

This agency, in carrying out its role of regulation and supervision, has the opportunity to continue to contribute immeasurably to the system's performance, the strengthening of the sound role of the banks, and the maintenance of good rapport with the Congress and in the Executive Branch. This is essential to the system.

Dedication

Continued dedication to proven cooperative and credit fundamentals and the concept of providing critical assistance to farmers through sound loans to their cooperatives will be necessary to maintain and build on the priceless system and Farm Credit heritage. The banks must never increase loan volume at the expense of soundness in their basic decisions. They must always remember the objectives for which they were created and the farmers and ranchers for whom they work.

All of these issues assume even greater significance when it is recalled that the banks are in a period of tremendous growth and change.

Appendix

CENTRAL BANK BOARD

For each of the bank's directors over the forty-two year period, a brief description is given of his key business activity. Generally this is limited to one business activity. A key role in a farmer cooperative such as service on the Board of a regional cooperative is cited. However, in general there is no mention of multiple roles, such as director of several cooperatives. An attempt was made to seek out active leadership roles in the Farm Credit System, such as being an officer or board member or a member of a key National Committee. No effort was made to identify work with one or more of the general national farm organizations. However, it was the purpose to mention active service in one of the national commodity organizations, the National Council of Farmer Cooperatives and as a trustee or officer of the American Institute of Cooperation. An attempt was made to keep the sketches concise. Since identity is the main purpose, the key roles are listed whether they occurred before, during or after service on the Central Bank Board.

Comments about the Board Chairmen in the government years are included in Chapter 3; in the years as a Farm Credit bank in Chapter 4. Comments on Dr. L. L. Boger are included in Chapter 7.

MEMBERS OF CENTRAL BANK BOARD, 1933-1974

F. W. Peck 1933-1935 Chairman
Cooperative Bank Commissioner. Deceased.

Thomas Cooper, Kentucky 1933-1951
Dean and Director, Agricultural College, University of Kentucky, Chief of Bureau of Agricultural Economics, U.S. Department of Agriculture. Member and Chairman of the Board of the Farm Credit Banks of Louisville. Deceased.

John D. Miller, Pennsylvania 1933-1944
Vice President and General Counsel of Dairymen's League Cooperative Association (now Dairylea Cooperative, Inc.), Pearl River, New York, and President, National Milk Producers Federation. He has been characterized as "The Father of the Capper-Volstead Act." Chairman of the National Milk Producers Federation committee which presented the bill to Congress. President of the predecessor organization to the National

Council of Farmer Cooperatives, Trustee of the American Institute of Cooperation. Deceased.

H. Lane Young, Georgia 1933-1940
President of the Citizens and Southern National Bank, Atlanta; regarded as one of the outstanding bankers of the South. Deceased.

H. E. Babcock, New York 1933-1940
One of the organizers, an incorporator and briefly Secretary of GLF (now Agway, Inc., Syracuse, New York) and later its general manager. Professor of Marketing at Cornell University and later Chairman of its Board of Trustees. President of the National Council of Farmer Cooperatives. Chairman of the Board of Trustees of the American Institute of Cooperation. Member of the Federal Farm Board. Deceased.

F. M. Hayner, New Mexico 1933-1938
Irrigated cotton grower and businessman in the El Paso, Texas area and President of Southwestern Irrigated Cotton Growers, El Paso. Deceased.

U. M. Dickey, Washington 1933-1937
General manager of United Dairymen's Association, Seattle and National Director of the National Milk Producers Federation. Deceased.

S. D. Sanders, Washington 1936-1947 Chairman
Cooperative Bank Commissioner. Deceased.

H. L. Kokernot, Texas 1937-1940
Rancher, businessman and President of Texas Livestock Marketing Association, Saginaw. Deceased.

Charles G. Henry, Tennessee 1938-1941
Cotton grower, organizer, and manager of the Mid-South Cotton Growers Association, Memphis. Member of the Board of Directors of the National Council of Farmer Cooperatives. Deceased.

James H. Lemmon, South Dakota 1940-1956
Raised sheep and was for years manager of the Lemmon, S.D. Produc-

tion Credit Association and President of the National Wool Marketing Corporation, Boston. Served on the Board of the National Council of Farmer Cooperatives. Deceased.

M. W. Thatcher, Minnesota 1940-1955
General Manager and an organizer of the Farmers Union Grain Terminal Association, St. Paul. Organizer and President of the National Federation of Grain Cooperatives.

O. O. Wolf, Kansas 1940-1944
Wheat farmer. Board member of his production credit association and that of Union Equity Co-Operative Exchange, Enid, Oklahoma. Member of the Board of Directors of the National Council of Farmer Cooperatives.

W. G. Wysor, Virginia 1941-1950
Organizer and General Manager of the Virginia Feed Service and its successor, Southern States Cooperative, Inc., Richmond. Member of the Board of Directors of the National Council of Farmer Cooperatives. Trustee of the American Institute of Cooperation. Chairman of the Board of the Federal Reserve Bank of Richmond.

Homer L. Brinkley, Louisiana 1944-1949
President and Executive Vice President of the National Council of Farmer Cooperatives. Extensive prior work in cooperative managment.

Leon A. Chapin, New York 1944-1953
Member of the executive committee and Treasurer of Dairymen's League Cooperative Association (now Dairylea Cooperative, Inc., Pearl River, New York, and a member of the Board of the Farm Credit Banks of Springfield. Member of the National Milk Producers Federation Executive Committee. Deceased.

J. E. Wells, Jr., South Dakota 1947-1948 Chairman
Cooperative Bank Commissioner. Deceased.

R. L. Farrington, Oklahoma 1949-1953 Chairman
Cooperative Bank Commissioner.

Henry G. Bennett, Oklahoma 1949-1951
President of Oklahoma Agriculture and Mechanics College (now Oklahoma State University) and the first administrator of the "Point 4 program," now AID, U.S. Department of State. Deceased.

Stephen Pace, Georgia 1951-1956
United States Congressman, influential in Agricultural legislation. His close working association with Congressman Clifford Hope of Kansas led to the saying "Pace, Hope and Parity." Deceased.

F. R. Wilcox, California 1952-1966
Chairman, 1956-1964
Deceased.

Marvin J. Briggs, Indiana 1953-1955
General Manager of Indiana Farm Bureau Cooperative Association, member and Chairman of the Board of the Farm Credit Banks of Louisville, member and Chairman of the Federal Farm Credit Board. Served on the Board of Directors of the National Council of Farmer Cooperatives. Deceased.

J. D. Lawrence, South Carolina 1954 Chairman
FCA Deputy Governor and Director of the Cooperative Bank Service.

Stanley H. Benham, New York 1954-1956
Member of the Executive Committee and President of Dairymen's League Cooperative Association (now Dairylea Cooperative, Inc., Pearl River, New York). Member of the National Milk Producers Association Executive Committee. Served on the Board of Directors of the National Council of Farmer Cooperatives.

Homer G. Smith, Maryland 1954-1955 Chairman
FCA Deputy Governor and Director of the Cooperative Bank Service.

O. E. Zacharias, Virginia 1955-1959
General Manager of Southern States Cooperative, Inc., Richmond. Served on the Board of Directors of the National Council of Farmer Cooperatives. Deceased.

James H. Dean, Kansas 1955-1968 Chairman, 1968

John D. Fehsenfeld, Missouri 1957-1960
General livestock farmer and President of National Livestock Producers Association, formerly of Chicago and now of Denver. Served on the Board of Directors of the National Council of Farmer Cooperatives. Deceased.

K. N. Probasco, Ohio 1957-1968 Chairman, 1965-1966

Wilmer Smith, Texas 1957-1965, 1972- Chairman 1976

Frank D. Stone, Minnesota 1957-1964
General Manager of Land O'Lakes Creameries, Inc. (now Land O'Lakes), Minneapolis. Member of National Milk Producers Federation Board of Directors, Executive Committee member and later Honorary Member of the Federation in 1968. Served on the Board of Trustees of the American Institute of Cooperation.

Julian B. Thayer, Connecticut 1959-1961
Poultryman and dairyman. Chairman of the Executive Committee and Director of Eastern States Farmers Exchange, Springfield, Massachusetts (now a part of Agway, Inc., Syracuse, New York), member and Chairman of the Board of the Farm Credit Banks of Springfield, member and Chairman of the Federal Farm Credit Board, and Chairman of the Commission on Agricultural Credit which functioned in 1969 and 1970.

Roland N. Benjamin, Pennsylvania 1961-1964
Organizer, President and executive secretary of Pennsylvania Farm Bureau Cooperative (now a part of Agway, Inc., Syracuse, New York). Member and chairman of the Board of the Farm Credit Banks of Baltimore.

Lorin T. Bice, Florida 1961-1963
Citrus grower. Manager of the Haines City Citrus Growers Association, Federal Land Bank Association Director, Production Credit Association Director and Vice President, member and Chairman of the Board of the

Farm Credit Banks of Columbia, member and Chairman of the Federal Farm Credit Board and member of Florida Citrus Commission.

A. L. Farnham, Missouri 1961-1966
General Manager of Producers Produce Co., Springfield and a member of the Board of the Farm Credit Banks of St. Louis. Deceased.

Oscar Heline, Iowa 1961
General farmer and stockman. President of Farmers' Grain Dealers Association of Iowa, Des Moines, and member and chairman of the Board of Farm Credit Banks of Omaha. Served on the Board of Directors of the National Council of Farmers Cooperatives.

William J. Holman, Idaho 1961-1963
Dairy farmer. Chairman of the Board of United Dairymen's Association, Seattle. Member and Chairman of the Board of the Farm Credit Banks of Spokane, and member of the Board of Directors of National Milk Producers Federation. Deceased.

C. R. Sayre, Mississippi 1961-1966
President and General Manager of Staple Cotton Cooperative Association, Staple Cotton Discount Corporation and Staple Cotton Services Association (AAL).

Frank J. Welch, Kentucky 1961
Dean, School of Agriculture, Mississippi State College and Director of Mississippi Experiment Station; Dean, College of Agriculture and Home Economics, and Director of Experiment Station, University of Kentucky; Assistant Secretary of Agriculture and member of the Board of Trustees, American Institute of Cooperation.

C. Brice Ratchford, Missouri 1961-1963
President, University of Missouri. Chairman of the Board of Trustees of the American Institute of Cooperation.

Luther W. Jennejahn, New York 1961-1967
Fruit grower. Member and Chairman of the Board of the Farm Credit Banks of Springfield and a member of the Federal Farm Credit Board.

Walter W. Peterson, Nebraska 1962-1967 Chairman, 1967

John T. Lesley, Florida 1963-1971 Chairman, 1971

Howard G. Diesslin, Indiana 1964-1966
Director, Cooperative Extension Service and Associate Dean of the School of Agriculture at Purdue University.

Don H. Phipps, Washington 1964-1968
General manager, Northwest Wholesale Inc., Wenatchee; member and Chairman of the Board of the Farm Credit Banks of Spokane. Served on the Board of the National Council of Farmer Cooperatives. Deceased.

J. Homer Remsberg, Maryland 1965-1968
Dairy farmer. President, Maryland and Virginia Milk Producers Association, member of the National Milk Producers Federation Board of Directors and the Federation's Treasurer. Member and Chairman of the Board of the Farm Credit Banks of Baltimore and a member and Chairman of the Federal Farm Credit Board. National Director and President of the Holstein-Friesian Association of America. Deceased.

Guido Schroeder, Wisconsin 1965-1970
Chairman, 1969-1970

Horace Smith, Texas 1966
Wheat farmer, Chairman of the Board of Producers Grain Corporation, Amarillo; member of the Board of the Farm Credit Banks of Houston, and active in the National Grain Producers Federation. Deceased.

M. E. Decherd, Texas 1966-1971
Cotton and grain farmer and economist. Instructor at the University of Houston.

Lawrence L. Boger, Michigan 1967-1971
Capital Committee.

H. Allan Segraves, Arkansas 1967-1969
Cotton producer. Chairman of Board of the Farm Credit Banks of St.

Louis. President of Home Oil Company and a Director of the Federal Land Bank Association at Oceola.

Owen Cooper, Mississippi 1967-1972
President and organizer of Mississippi Chemical Corporation, Yazoo City.

Glen R. Harris, California 1967-1975, Chairman 1972-73

Milford M. Beeghly, Iowa 1968-1973
Livestock and grain farmer. President of Farmers Grain Dealers Association of Iowa, Des Moines and member and Chairman of the Board of the Farm Credit Banks of Omaha. Served on the Board of Directors of the National Council of Farmer Cooperatives. Member of the Board of Trustees of the American Institute of Cooperation.

Chester E. Goodfield, Massachusetts 1968-1970
Dairy farmer. Member of the Board of Eastern States Farmers Exchange (now a part of Agway, Inc., Syracuse, New York), Director of Federal Land Bank and Production Credit Associations, and member of the Board of the Farm Credit Banks of Springfield.

William T. Steele, Virginia 1968-1973
General Manager of Southern States Cooperative Association, Inc., Richmond.

Melvin A. Ensley, Washington 1968-
Chairman 1974-1975

William Kenneth Miller, Indiana 1969-1974
Assistant General Manager of Indiana Farm Bureau Cooperative Association, Inc., Indianapolis. Member and Chairman of the Board of the Farm Credit Banks of Louisville. Served on the Board of Trustees of the American Institute of Cooperation.

Ben Swigart, Oklahoma 1969-1973
Dairy farmer and wheat farmer. Production Credit Association Director and member and Chairman of the Board of the Farm Credit Banks of

Wichita. Member of the Commission on Agricultural Credit which was active in 1969 and 1970. Deceased.

Hilmer E. Albrecht, Illinois 1970-
General Manager of Randolph Service Company, Sparta. Member and Chairman of the Board of the Farm Credit Banks of St. Louis.

Darrell D. Moseson, Minnesota 1971-
Senior Vice President, Finance, CENEX, South St. Paul. Member and Chairman of the Board of the Farm Credit Banks of St. Paul.

Kenneth M. Noble, New York 1971-1973
Dairy and general farmer. Production Credit Association President, member of the Board of the Farm Credit Banks of Springfield, and a Director of Agway, Inc., Syracuse.

Howard F. Robinson, North Carolina 1971-1975
Director, Research Administration, and Professor of Agricultural Economics, North Carolina Agricultural and Technical State University.

A. J. Haynes, North Carolina 1972-
President and General Manager of FCX Inc., Raleigh. Member of the Board and Chairman of the Farm Credit Banks of Columbia. Served on the Board of Directors of the National Council of Farmer Cooperatives.

Joseph A. Kyser, Alabama 1973-
Catfish and cattle producer. Member of the Board of Farm Credit Banks of New Orleans.

Henry W. Bibus, New Jersey 1974-
Grain and vegetable grower. Vice Chairman of the Board of Directors of Agway, Syracuse, New York, and member of the Board of the Farm Credit Banks of Springfield.

James R. Isleib, Kansas 1974
Land Bank Commissioner, Farm Credit Administration. Special loan representative for the Wichita and Central Banks. Member and Chair-

man of the Board of the Farm Credit Banks of Wichita.

Fred J. Ludwig, Iowa 1974-
General farmer and feeder. President of Farmers Grain Dealers Association of Iowa, Des Moines. Member and Chairman of the Board of the Farm Credit Banks of Omaha. Member of the Board of the U.S. Feed Grains Council and a Director of Farmers Export Company, Ama, Louisiana.

John W. Stone, West Virginia 1974-
Livestock farmer. Member and Chairman of the Board of Southern States Cooperative, Inc., Richmond, Virginia. Member and Chairman of the Board of the Farm Credit Banks of Baltimore.

ROLE OF THE CENTRAL BANK AND ITS CREDIT STAFF ON PARTICIPATION LOANS IN 1974

The crucial importance of sound credit administration in the Banks for Cooperatives System and the unique role of the Central Bank in the system led to the decision to include as a supplement the following statement, prepared as a guide for internal use, to promote better understanding.

The Central Bank has accomplished a unique and difficult function which provided a different kind of job satisfaction and a sense of accomplishment from that provided in District Banks, which work directly with cooperatives in the lending function. With its tremendous dollar involvement in some loans and the critical role the bank must play in many instances, the qualifications for key credit staff are exacting, and adequate staffing is one of the most important requirements.

Over more than four decades, the Banks for Cooperatives System has built an excellent record for sound and constructive credit service to the farmer cooperatives of the nation. This is a record of thirteen banks under the supervision of the Farm Credit Administration. The twelve District Banks carry the greatest part of the load and thus need most of the personnel. The Central Bank works closely with all of the District Banks, and it has been pleased with its relationships in its role as a bank of participation.

The Central Bank, as one of the thirteen banks, has established on its own an enviable record in the extension of credit both in its one-time role as a direct lender to cooperatives and later as a bank of participation. Many of the strong large cooperatives of the nation would not have achieved their present status without the availability of this service. These cooperatives may have obtained loans which would not have been available from other lenders, and the results are that major strides have been made in aiding producers to establish and maintain markets, reduce their costs and increase their income.

In its entire history the Central Bank has never taken a loss on the $2.1 billion of loans which it made direct to cooperatives and through 1974 had sustained only two losses on the $21.5 billion of credit on participations. The losses offset by recoveries resulted in net chargeoffs of some $200,000 over a forty-two year period.

Admittedly the Central Bank in 1974 had a few serious problem participation loans. Forthright reports had been made to the Board on a timely basis on all problems as they had developed. Also, cooperating with District Banks, aggressive action had been taken to help work them out. In addition, valuation reserves ($14 million) deemed to be appropriate in relation to these specific accounts had been established. Thus, the bank presented an honest and objective financial statement.

It is especially significant that the bank's Credit Department is comprised of professional credit men of demonstrated competence consistent with their assignments.

Perhaps a few words should be said about its concept in 1974 of a competent, professional credit man as applied to the bank. The objective of credit expertise is sound judgment. This requires good appraisal of the economic aspects of a venture, its feasibility from a cooperative viewpoint and accurate evaluation of management in all of its phases—production, marketing and finance, member and public relations.

To a considerable degree, loans are made based on appraisals of people, and thus there must be an ability to understand and rather accurately judge people, whether at the producer, Board or the management level.

The Central Bank has an added essential appraisal which relates to the credit philosophy and approach of the District Bank which will be servicing the loan and the strength and depth of its staff.

In the case of both borrowers and banks, profound changes in basic philosophy often occur seemingly suddenly. Often it is not possible to evaluate the changes for a considerable period until performance can be observed.

It is especially important that the bank's credit officers, cooperating with District Banks, take a positive approach and seek to help find a way to structure a sound loan in situations which may be deemed to be borderline. Its purpose is not to reject loans but to find ways that basically sound projects can be financed on appropriate terms.

It is imperative that its credit officers be able to function appropriately in a participation situation and be able to work competently with District Bank officials with firmness as the situation requires and yet in a spirit of give and take which is essential to good working relationships and in avoiding a situation where the Central Bank gets out in front except where its interests so require.

To meet these requirements, its credit officers must have a sound basic background of education, training and experience; a judicious temperament; a high level of analytical ability; competence in understanding complicated financial and operating statements; the ability to make sound projections; preferably some degree of competence in what we might call auditing techniques and the ability to attend to meticulous detail as required, particularly in relation to the sometimes highly involved basic loan agreements and side agreements—for example, with participating Commercial Banks or participating District Banks. These attributes must be coupled with a high level of knowledge of credit instruments, commercial law, sound credit principles, along with appropriate ratios to serve as general guidelines and the bank's credit concepts.

The end result is the capacity:

1. to tailor loan agreements and the structuring of loans to the many varying situations;
2. to be effective as loan negotiations are in progress and when the loan agreements are consummated;
3. to perform adequately as there is a need for normal Central Bank overview of the servicing of loans; and
4. to be effective should loans get into difficulties.

There is another significant overall requirement. The bank's credit staff must have diversified background as to education and training and agricultural industry knowledge and must be representative of the major agricultural areas of the nation, yet must function as a team.

Of great importance also is the fact that the mix of subjective judgments among the credit staff provides a good system of checks and balances, which is of paramount importance to loan service. This is needed to avoid unsound or prejudiced one-man decisions either in agreeing to or disagreeing with a District Bank's recommendation and in reaching decisions as to proper approach in problem situations, including determinations of when outside technical help should be utilized.

Because of the complexity of these requirements, it takes a significant number of years of intensive credit experience for a competent, well-educated and trained individual with all the other qualifications to become a top-level professional credit man consistent with the bank's needs.

The Central Bank occupies a difficult position. It often described its job as one which could not be done. But it is of great importance that it be done because the combination of prime district responsibility for negotiating and for servicing the participation loans, when appropriately carried out as is normally the case, supplemented by an effective Central Bank serving as a working partner reviewing the credit package for acceptability adds to the local knowledge, the broad overview, and a checkpoint and gives excellent results in credit service.

The Central Bank may have difficulties in those instances where major differences of view develop as to the proper approach or where it encounters resistance to being recognized as a working partner. Then the Central Bank is placed on its mettle and an adequate staff of credit professionals becomes critical.

The Central Bank's delicate situation at times results from its basic commitment to the concept of strong District Banks and its sincere desire and responsibility to see that they not be overwhelmed by the Central Bank; and yet, on the other hand, its difficult position in instances when, in its judgment, the District Bank which has the responsibility for servicing a participation loan may not be performing adequately.

Returning to a system view, the overall performance over some forty-two years has been impressive. In 1974, there were a few participation accounts with serious problems, but it is clear that, in a lending operation such as that of the system, there inevitably will be problem loans. Credit expertise and sound servicing will not prevent occasional management lapses, adverse economic or labor developments, problems with governmental regulatory agencies or need for pollution control or occasional lapses in credit administration.